Plane Thoughts On Parish Ministry

A Flight Plan For Being An Effective And Faithful Pastor

Jerry L. Schmalenberger

CSS Publishing Company, Inc.
Lima, Ohio

PLANE THOUGHTS ON PARISH MINISTRY

Scripture quotations are from the *Good News Bible,* in Today's English Version. Copyright (c) American Bible Society 1966, 1971, 1976. Used by permission.

Library of Congress Cataloging-In-Publication Data

Schmalenberger, Jerry L.
  Plane thoughts on parish ministry : a flight plan for being an effective and faithful pastor / by Jerry L. Schmalenberger.
     p.   cm.
  ISBN 1-55673-599-5
  1. Clergy—Office. 2. Pastoral theology. 3. Lutheran Church—Clergy. 4. Pastoral theology—Lutheran Church. I. Title.
BV660.2.S35   1994
253—dc20   93-38127
                                                                    CIP

ISBN 1-55673-599-5   PRINTED IN U.S.A.

To the Pacific Lutheran Theological Seminary graduating class of 1993 who made the test flight with me.

Table Of Contents

Pastor As Preacher: Proclaiming The Good News

Pastor As Administrator: Organizing For Mission

Pastor As Program Resource: Maintaining Mission Emphasis

When To Leave The Parish: Signs It's Time To Move On

Foreword And Acknowledgements

This book evolved over a period of several years. As I flew to my many speaking engagements as president of Pacific Lutheran Theological Seminary, I jotted down outlines of the thoughts I had about my 29 years as a parish pastor.

The content of the book came primarily from those outlines written while travelling on airplanes, hence the title, *Plane Thoughts On Parish Ministry*. The outlines were then fleshed out and given as lectures in my courses in Discipling, Evangelism, Stewardship and Ministry for senior students at Pacific Lutheran Theological Seminary.

Some of the thoughts were written in preparation for conducting continuing education courses for pastors throughout the United States. Others were roughed out as I prepared discussion material for seminary interns and their supervisors in parishes across the U.S.

Each of the chapters was read by the students in one of my senior classes and then discussed. This discussion provided additional helpful insights and perceptions on these subjects that need to be dealt with in parish ministry.

Except for a couple of chapters, the manuscript was mailed out to the following readers, who then supplied to me their suggestions and critiques: The Reverend Kelly Denton-Borhaug, pastor of Golden Gate Lutheran Church, San Francisco, California; the Reverend Dr. Don Hillerich, pastor of St. Paul Lutheran Church, Sarasota, Florida; the Reverend Dr. Robert Hock, pastor of St. John's Lutheran Church, Winter Park, Florida; Mrs. Anna-Marie Klein, Kirkland, Washington, lay person and advisor to Center for Lutheran Church Growth and Mission, Pacific Lutheran Theological Seminary; the Reverend Dr. Ronald Lavin, pastor and evangelist, Our Saviour's Lutheran Church, Tucson, Arizona; the Reverend Dr. Raymond LeBlanc, pastor, First Lutheran

Church, Carson City, California; the Reverend Dr. Robert Miller, Bishop of Pacifica Synod, ELCA; the Reverend Susan Nachtigal, Instructor of Christian Education and Spirituality, Pacific Lutheran Theological Seminary; the Reverend Muriel Peterson, Mission developer and pastor of Community of Hope Lutheran Church, Wilsonville, Oregon; the Reverend Dr. David E. Ullery, pastor of All Saints Lutheran Church, Worthington, Ohio; the Reverend Maria Valenzuela, pastor of Cristo Rey Centro Luterano, El Paso, Texas; the Reverend Robert Winkel, pastor of Our Savior's Lutheran Church, Everett, Washington; the Reverend William Wong, Director for Commission for Multicultural Ministries, ELCA. Dr. Michael Aune, my colleague and Associate Professor of Worship, helped me with the chapter on Worship Leadership; my friend, Win Arn, of Monrovia, California, is always gracious in allowing me to quote from his vital *Growth Report* newsletter on church growth.

Special thanks to my faithful administrative assistant, Wendy Eilers, and my wife, Carol Walthall Schmalenberger, for typing and editing the manuscript.

While parish pastors could not agree completely on such subjects as are dealt with in this volume, certainly there is enough depth on each subject that it can stimulate thought, focus and further meaningful discussion on how and why we do our ministries in the parish and in the world.

Paul wrote: "God, in God's mercy, has given us this ministry, and so we do not become discouraged." — 2 Corinthians 4:1.

The author outlines "Plane Thoughts" on a United 727 flight.

**The author outlines "Plane Thoughts"
on a United 727 flight.**

Parish Pastor:

Getting Started

The Office Of Parish Pastor

I was sitting in 11-A on Southwest Airlines flight #1595 from San Antonio, Texas, to Oakland, California. The man next to me asked, "Well, Father, how's the God business?" Stunned for a moment, I simply mumbled, "It's going pretty well." But I would have liked to tell him the truth, as I see it! Across our land there is a strong anti-clericalism that abounds in our church and congregations that is eating away at the very office of being a parish pastor. I think some of that attitude comes from a general lack of respect for anyone in authority right now, because we have failed to meet expectations, and the ridicule we often experience from the secular world for the office of parish pastor. Certainly acquiescing to an informality that gives up using our title or even dressing to look like a pastor has contributed to this, as well.

Our clergy's morale is very low. Some of this comes from being pastors in congregations that have plateaued, are declining, or, at best, are in a state of passivity. Our society and congregational members are at a higher level of frustration than they used to be and regularly take out their frustration by attacking those who fill the pastoral office. In addition, more and more of our congregational members have acquiesced to a self-centered, secular individualism and they are very nervous about job security, income, feeling used by their government, and are afraid and insecure in their present position.

Perhaps the problem runs deeper than that. I probably should have told the fellow who asked me about the "God business" the truth. Many clergy are not as certain as they used to be of the relevance and importance of what we do and who we are in our communities. Perhaps our self-esteem has declined and we have become suspicious of the church at large, like many of our laity have. Clergy who are middle-aged, white males have experienced a further reduction in self-esteem as the church works valiantly to be inclusive and seeks women

13

and persons of color and primary language other than English to serve in the church across the land.

When doctors, dentists, professional athletes, and public school teachers began to emphasize their professional status, we clergy fell right into that trap and have talked about it constantly since. At about the same time, the church took on a very corporate methodology of organizing and carrying out its business. We clergy became "hired hands" to serve members. In all that emphasis on being "professional" and "corporate," we lost (or at least diluted) our sense of divine call to word and sacrament ministry. Over the last several years a number of clergy have been carrying out their pastoral role embarrassed to be spiritual leaders and perhaps not even knowing how to be religious people! The laity have sensed this spiritual crisis and have not taken us as seriously as they might have if there were more depth to our faith.

The language describing "ministry of laity in daily life" may have contributed further deterioration of the pastoral office. We need to come up with some different verbiage so the clergy can keep their sense of uniqueness and high calling to the ministry of word and sacrament, while not demoting or demeaning the appropriate and responsible role of the laity.

I have no doubt that one of the major factors contributing to the decline of respect for the pastoral office has been the past teaching of clergy to do what was called "enabling," or "leading from the middle" philosophy of leadership. The church needs leaders, not just enablers! Congregations are hungry for visionary parish pastors who will lead in a risk-taking fashion, encouraging others to follow.

In commenting on the leader in the secular world Burt Nanus writes: "Leaders live the vision by making all their actions and behaviors consistent with it and by creating a sense of urgency and passion for its attainment." (*Visionary Leadership: Creating a Compelling Sense of Direction for Your Organization,* Jossey-Bass Management Series, HB Printing, 1992, San Francisco)

The media's portrayal of the clergy as fools and incompetents hasn't helped our image either! Numerous exposés of some real manipulators of people on the televangelist circuit have made the perception of clergy even worse.

In a December 1992 article in the *Christian Century* headed "Poll finds clergy image dips to new low," the following was reported:

> *"There was a time when the clergy was at the top of the list of American occupations ranked by the public as having high standards of honesty and ethics,"* *the Gallup-related center said in its publication* Emerging Trends.
>
> *The report said that positive ratings for clergy peaked in 1985, when two persons in three ranked them very highly. But by 1988, when the scandals involving Jim Bakker, Jimmy Swaggart, and other televangelists began hitting the newspapers, favorable ratings dropped to 60% and for the first time clergy trailed pharmacists in the annual poll.*
>
> *"Further declines have continued to occur to this year when public confidence in the clergy has reached its lowest point ever, with just a bare majority now rating them 'very high' (15%) or 'high' (39%) in honesty and ethical standards,"* *the report noted.*

It's little wonder so many of us clergy feel a reduced sense of worthiness and importance in our sacred calling!

If I'd thought that fellow in 11-B really wanted to know about the God business, I'd probably have unloaded on him further. There seems to be a mentality right now among a whole generation in our congregations of measuring the effectiveness of the pastoral ministry by whether their needs are met and they are entertained as they would like, rather than by whether they have been properly discipled and have the word proclaimed and sacraments provided to them so they might be empowered to carry on their discipleship in the world.

At this point I'd probably have told my seat mate that Paul, who experienced many struggles in his ministry, wrote in

2 Corinthians 4:1, "Therefore, since through God's mercy we have this ministry, we do not lose heart." In light of the above, it is difficult not to lose heart, but there are some steps which I believe can make a great difference in helping us clergy regain our self-esteem and sense of importance and urgency in the ministry we do, while remaining a humble servant in our kingdom work.

We need to do some work in reclaiming the title of "pastor," "preacher," and "ordained minister," as something extremely important and an office to which God calls *some*.

And let's put less emphasis on "professional" and much more on the called clergy as set apart to *serve* people. I know the dangers of that, but I think it more dangerous to have a watered down office of word and sacrament that simply is of no significance to lay people to be served and empowered for their discipleship or to the one who fills the office and must serve.

Certainly we need to look at theological education in a way that evaluates how we might better enhance the spiritual life of those who aspire to be clergy and train them how to be effective spiritual guides to their own people. We need to consider new ways to live out the authority which comes with our office of parish pastor. We cannot return to former and lost models of pastoral authority. An increase on the emphasis of prayer and the spiritual dimension of the call committee (not *search* committee!) in local congregations can help, as well.

We also ought to make sure we give a clear and distinctive presentation of the pastoral office to our youth and new members as they join the congregation.

A more confident, healthy, self-esteemed pastor will be much more likely to affirm and empower a ministry of the laity. Perhaps we could use the word discipleship for that which the laity do and reserve the word "ministry" more for what the minister who is ordained to word and sacrament does.

The Reverend William Wong of Chicago writes in response to this manuscript: "Another question which needs to be raised is the role of the church institution in supporting its pastors.

16

Are the pastors being cared for, visited by judicatory heads or staff, provided with and encouraged to participate in continuing education, surrounded by a climate which encourages collegial relations with other pastors, versus a climate of a 'lone ranger,' encouraged to be spiritual leaders, spiritual people and brought together for renewal?''

If I had said all these things to that fellow who sat in 11-B, I am certain he would have asked a flight attendant if he could move! (It might have been hard for him to find a flight attendant because they probably would have left the area, as well, as I entered into such a tirade!) It is just that I have a strong sense that the pastoral office and how it is perceived is in serious trouble in our church and we need to take dramatic steps in order to affirm, empower and equip our clergy with spiritual depth. With an increased sense of call, self-esteem and spirit power, they might be much more effective in carrying out their ministry. What if you had gotten the question in 11-C? What would be your answer?

Not every pastor will serve a "successful" large congregation. Not every pastor is gifted for "success" as often defined by numbers and dollars. We need to find a way to balance effectiveness, numbers and dollars with faithfulness and spiritual growth. God rejoices in the variety of gifts in the people called to be parish pastors. Perhaps the following pages will offer suggestions of a very practical nature which will help do pastoral ministry well, or affirm that it already is being done well, and thus bring an increased sense of value to pastors who are trying so hard to be faithful to God's call. No pastor could do all of them, but there might be a few in each chapter that will help.

The Pastor's Spiritual Health

When preparing for a take-off the flight attendant explains that if needed, the oxygen mask will fall in front of the passenger if it is needed. The attendant instructs us: "... if traveling with small children, put your mask on first, then help your child." The reasoning is obvious, just as it is obvious to me that we ought to care for our own spiritual health before trying to help others with theirs.

One of the most important factors in determining a congregation's faithfulness and a pastor's ability to lead that congregation in spiritual maturation and mission in the world is the pastor's spiritual health. Here are some suggestions on how we clergy can keep fit in our own spirituality.

We need a time every day for meditation, prayer and study of the scriptures. This needs to be different from that work which we do preparing to teach Bible studies and our regular preaching. Almost all congregations will deeply respect the pastor who announces the time period each day when he/she will be in devotions and meditation. One half to one hour ought to do it, and the secretary can protect you during that time of deepening your spiritual life. Because of congregational expectations of pastors to be their spiritual directors and because of the challenge of serving as a pastor, pastors must have this time of spiritual deepening and enrichment each day. Many claim that a weekly text study group helps fill this need.

Pastors need a time each month when they can hear the word proclaimed and receive Holy Communion from someone else. It ought to be a time when we are not in charge or responsible for any part of it. In a larger community, that might be a weekday service at another Christian church. In a smaller community, it may even be a richer experience if we could find a different denomination in which we could receive the sacrament and worship at least once a month. It's just impossible to have a quality worship experience while we're thinking what we need to do next in leading our own congregation's worship. If we go to a different denomination's worship service, it also is a witness to the fact that we do have an ecumenical approach to the faith and we do see ourselves as a part of a larger family of God.

We all need our own pastor. We need that person who can be a confessor for us — someone who cares about our spiritual health and nurture and who doesn't have anything to do with our career. This may rule out bishops and superintendents. Some try hard to be a pastor to pastors, but their ability due to schedules and geography is often as much a barrier as the perceived power of a judicatory head. While in theory the church says its leaders should be a pastor to pastors, it's just not possible to have that kind of quality spiritual direction from one we believe has so much power over our present and next call.

Every pastor needs a pastoral relations committee or a mutual ministry committee (or something similar). This group would be comprised of the very faithful and often elder wise people of the congregation whom we trust. At monthly meetings with this committee, they can interpret the congregation's feelings to us and we can open up to them our feelings and struggles and victories which can be a beautiful experience and often save our skin when we would otherwise move into a real time of conflict. There must be a mutual understanding about confidentiality in this committee.

We all need a time away from the parish of at least two weeks in duration for study and relaxation. No matter how much of an accomplished theologian we are and how well our ministry is going, we need to pause for a couple of weeks each year to step back and get the larger picture. We need that time which brings things into perspective and can be introspective and also visioning. Continuing education is a must because just keeping up with the fast changing information and methodology of pastoral ministry means continually retooling and reorganizing as we do our work of a called pastor. It helps to have continuing education written into the call with a promise of budget funds to carry it out. The trend seems to be toward an agreement with the congregation for a pastoral sabbatical, as well.

Try keeping a journal. It can be a very spiritual experience. Just the discipline of writing each day of our spiritual struggles and joys and the ability to look back over that journal to keep our proper perspective makes it very valuable. There are different kinds of journaling. One can be simply noting those things that you observe which are usable as metaphors in your preaching. Another way is to be much more introspective and treat the journal more like a diary, logging your spiritual ups and downs as you progress and mature in your spiritual life. Either, or both, can help bring a new awareness of God's presence in our lives and in the world in which we live.

Once a week we ought to have fun with our family, an experience not church related. Some pastors simply write-in their family time each week into their regular schedule. This time ought to be full of play and laughter. If single, we ought to find someone else in the community or outside the community who can enjoy with us that one evening saved or that Saturday afternoon that is reserved. There is a certain playfulness about God and the faith and we need to keep that rehearsed and relived over and over. There is great therapy in laughter and foolishness and we need not give that up simply because we are ordained into a very serious vocation.

A pastor who is perceived to be "too busy" tends to be a barrier for members interrupting his/her "busy schedule." Be careful about overly restrictive hours of availability, however; it can backfire if interpreted as the "only hours" you will come to their side if needed.

Do build into your calendar a renewal of your sense of call. This might mean reading a book on the theology of call at least once a year, or it could mean a conference on the subject or it could be our own writing about it. Consider getting together annually the call committee who brought you to the congregation and making that a deeply spiritual prayer group which reminds you periodically to what and by whom you are called.

Some pastors find it very helpful to discuss their call with a spiritual director or respected colleague.

If married, we must have quality time with our spouse and children or grandchildren. That means getting away from the parish and the church building, divorcing ourselves enough from the daily routine that we can concentrate on relating directly to spouse and kids. It's hand-holding time, it's hugging time, it's time when intimate conversation is shared and cherished. You will probably be a better pastor if you take the full vacation time and weekly day off.

We all need an annual medical checkup. We all must practice a program of daily exercise, good diet and frequent checkups of blood pressure and weight. The Reverend Kelly Denton-Borhaug of San Francisco writes: "Jogging for me is a time of solitude, mental and physical prayer." The Reverend Robert Winkel of Everett, Washington, adds: "I find physical exercise a component of spiritual health, since health is holistic." When we step into the pulpit we are athletes for God — the best communicators are often those who are in the best physical (as well as spiritual) shape. We owe it to ourselves, our family, and especially to the God who calls us to be good stewards of our body and our health. It pays big dividends in our morale and in the way we present the gospel with vigor and gusto to all those who will listen.

Before retiring each night, it's important that we assume a different posture and thank God for all that we have been able to do and receive that day. It helps us sleep, it puts us in tune with the Almighty who has so well cared for us, and it brings into our psyche that wonderful peace that only God can give. Some believe that you can pray on the run. I'm sure you can. However, I am convinced that folding hands, closing eyes and kneeling helps us even better to concentrate and communicate with and listen to the Almighty. Pastor Robert Winkel comments: "What is important is to have a place and posture that puts one in touch with God and the center of our being."

21

Pastor Susan Nachtigal, instructor in Christian Education at Pacific Lutheran Theological Seminary and former parish pastor at St. John's Lutheran Church, Sacramento, California, comments: "Sometimes, I feel there is a prevailing attitude among clergy that says 'we have it the worst of any profession' . . . 'we are the ones who work the hardest' . . . 'we are the ones who care the most.' Sometimes it seems as though clergy play the game of 'whoever has the most struggles, wins!' I think that clergy need to get rid of this victim role. Presently, we seem to support each other in this victim role, rather than holding each other accountable. Yes, it is a struggle . . . the demands are great . . . but each pastor must ask him or herself, 'what am I doing to maintain the necessary balance?' To ignore this discipline ends up being self-serving."

St. Paul wrote to Timothy, his son in the ministry: "If you give these instructions to the brothers and sisters you will be a good servant of Christ Jesus, as you feed yourself spiritually on the words of faith and of the true teaching which you have followed . . . keep yourself in training for a godly life." — 1 Timothy 4:6 and 7b.

A mechanic who drives a wreck of a car in need of repair, a house painter who lives in a home with paint peeling off the siding, or a medical doctor who is overweight, smokes, and is generally out of shape, is not the kind of person we would want to seek out for help in his or her profession. Our congregants also are best able to receive help from us in their spiritual struggles if we keep our spiritual health at its very best.

The First Few Days In The Parish

Those first couple of weeks in a new ministry (called the honeymoon) when you are looked over by the new congregation, community and larger church organization are very critical to the remainder of our ministry, wherever God has called us to be pastor. Mrs. Anna-Marie Klein, our lay reader, writes: "A pastor has many opportunities in the first year in a parish that do not happen again. And for the newly ordained, there are some advantages during the first call. For example, a pastor in a first ministry can understandably admit — 'I am listening and learning.' " The following are some thoughts I have on those first few days in the new parish as I have recorded them on United flight #1138 from San Francisco to Seattle.

Of course, the size and location of the new congregation we are beginning to serve will alter the priorities we set about what to do the first couple of weeks. An assistant pastorate in a large city will call for very different priorities than a small urban or rural solo pastorate.

It helps to know well the history of your new congregation and of the community in which the congregation is located. Begin to use some of those local stories in your sermons right away. This will give you credibility and will communicate to your congregation and community that you know and accept their heritage and plan to be a part of them. These stories about people and places in the community can be discovered at the local library in a county history, from members as we visit them, at the genealogical society (often by those who work there), or at the county seat court house lawn through the people who sit on those benches and are always anxious to relate past legends, heroes and heroines, and mysteries of places in the area.

Subscribing to the local newspaper ahead of the time you arrive at the new parish will help you get a feel for the milieu of the area. Be sure to read the letters to the editor, school board notes, chamber of commerce reports and so forth, and the editorial page, which will often inform you about the strident issues being debated.

Visit the patriarchs and matriarchs and a select few of the older shut-ins of the congregation right away. These are the individuals who have given time or wealth or both to the congregation. You might call them the people who have the power to withhold permission and can influence congregational decisions. These folks have given a lot of their life to the congregation's mission and ministry and it is important to honor them right away by making a visit in their home or the retirement center where they live. Word will rapidly spread throughout the congregation that you have taken this first step.

It's always important to be known and understood by the religion editor of the local paper. Call up and make an appointment to visit and then take along your picture and biography. Ask that person how she or he wants news written and what is news for that paper. The smaller the paper the more likelihood that they will pay attention to you and print your news. Smaller papers especially like good art with the stories submitted to them.

In smaller communities, you can make a visit to the mayor to identify yourself and simply become acquainted stating the fact that you want to be a part of the community and a good citizen. In larger communities, visit your local city or county representative. Stop off at the Chamber of Commerce office and introduce yourself, as well. Such an office often can help you better understand the issues and opportunities of your parish and are also good sources of local information.

Inspect the buildings of your congregation within the first few days you are there. Take along some lay people (especially members responsible for maintenance, buildings and property) and walk around carefully looking for some kind of drastic cosmetic maintenance you can do right away. (Be careful not to give the impression you do not approve of what they have.) This might be painting the main doors red or rebuilding or refurbishing the church's sign boards. It might be as simple as getting the walls of the restrooms repainted or planting trees or flowers for outside appearance. These little immediate victories communicate to the congregation that you take seriously the stewardship of all the resources and that your arrival has heralded a new day.

Find ways to identify those inactive members of the congregation (such as attendance records, financial records, communion records, conversation with the parish secretary) and devise a strategy to welcome them. Upon the arrival of a new pastor some of the people, who have not liked the former pastor or experienced some kind of anxiety-producing event and anger and moved away from the congregation's vitality and life, will venture back to take a look at you and see if you're the kind of person they might like. It's crucial that these people not be eliminated from your membership list before your arrival. It's even more crucial that you map out a strategy to contact them and invite them back into the congregation's activities without any censure or blame and especially any feeling of guilt because they have been gone.

Check with the altar guild president or whatever title is given to that dedicated saint of the congregation who cares for the chancel and altar. These are usually deeply spiritual people who have given their life to the congregation with little appreciation voiced for it. Spend time with them, get to know about their motivation for such dedicated service, and find a way to acknowledge their work over these many years. Institute a luncheon just for them. They will appreciate the attention and fellowship. Meet with the altar guild members at one of their meetings.

If you've moved into a small community, visit the local funeral directors you'll have to be working with at the time of death of your members and gently, but firmly, set down for them what your funeral practices will be. This is much easier done before you have the first funeral service with them.

Pay attention to the folks like the church janitor, secretaries, financial secretary, and that large array of volunteers who work so faithfully and may not have had any recognition for it for a long time. Let them know that you know of their efforts and you want to support them in every way possible.

Stake out your prayer time. I've never seen a congregation that resented their spiritual leader having time designated each day for his or her own spiritual life. Depending on what kind of lifestyle you live, this can often be an early morning hour when it is simply understood that you are reading the scripture, praying and meditating upon God's purposes for you and your congregation. If you have a secretary, that person can protect you during that time. If in a larger congregation with a staff, a time for devotions with them should be set as well. Folks will have deep respect for your daily working at being a spiritual person and you will find that time some of the most enriching that you have.

Take time right away to review with your governing board and publish your preferences for baptisms, weddings and funerals. After you've performed some, it's very difficult to do this, as you may very well hurt those for whom you've already conducted these rites of the church. Let your people know right away what your policy is concerning perquisites given for pastoral acts. I believe it brings even more respect for the office of pastor if you simply announce that you do not receive perquisites from members for any pastoral acts because you are paid adequately to be their pastor. In some areas, checks are automatically handed to the clergy. You can set a policy that it will go to the church, a special discretionary fund, and so forth. You can announce in writing that if people really want to show their appreciation by giving money for what you have done, you would like it given to your church's World Hunger fund, pastor's discretionary fund, benevolence, or to your own seminary from which you graduated.

In smaller communities, a visit to the hospital administrator where you will be making your calls helps immensely in carrying out those calls in the days ahead. Stop by the chaplain's office at the hospital, if there is one, and learn where you can hang your hat and coat, park your car, and when you have access to intensive care, coronary care, and other

26

restricted areas. Offer to help them in their ministries and explore how you might work together in the community. Chaplains and hospital administrators will deeply appreciate the respect you pay to them and this will help you immensely in the days ahead.

Surprise the community by attending a local high school sports event, class play or similar activity. Try to arrange a visit to the high school principal and counselor. This shows that you are planning to be a good citizen in the community and that you consider important all the areas of your parish to which you are expected to minister. If one exists, attend the local ministerium meeting.

In order to communicate your concern for the disenfranchised of the community, you might consider joining the NAACP's local chapter, seeking out the Urban League for membership, going up to volunteer in a homeless shelter. It isn't at all necessary that these community good works be affiliated with your denomination. Find out if there are community organizations or neighborhood associations located near the church. These are vital groups to connect with and show hospitality toward as your ministry begins. In fact, it will communicate your ecumenical spirit if you take these steps across denominational lines right away as you begin your ministry.

Don't forget to care for your family during this time of transition. Take time to settle in your own home.

The above suggestions provide a number of ways to get started so that you can communicate the kind of ministry you expect to carry out and introduce your personality to the community and your congregation. Although their motivation, in many cases, seems more political than theological, they will get you off to a good start as one of God's called people to serve in the office of pastor in that location.

I had a professor in Hamma Divinity School at Wittenberg University, Dr. Willard Allbeck, who admonished his students to remember that we are not underpaid our first couple of years in the parish ministry. He claimed we should pay the congregation for the training they gave us! His point is still valid. You can grow and mature a great deal if you are willing to listen to your people.

Parish Sacred Cows

There are special items, issues and people that clergy soon find are of special significance in almost any congregation. While they are tough to change, it can be done with planning and careful thought as to the best strategy. It may seem a bit irreverent to call them "sacred cows," but that term communicates their status, especially in older congregations, or younger ones made up of people who have a long-time history of involvement in the congregation. I'm sure that you will be able to list additional ones you have run up against in your ministry, but here are some that almost every church can identify.

Watch out for that **American flag** in the chancel! While we can find many good theological and liturgical reasons to relocate or get rid of it, it most often is a very symbolic item which can be moved only with a lot of pain. Where people do not move beyond a "civil religion," they thus do not understand the subtleties between representative symbols placed in the chancel of our church buildings. Especially those members who have fought in wars for which the flag holds a special significance, it is very difficult to convince them or explain the global perspective of the Christian faith and the need to move from a parochial narrowness to a much wider view of God's family worldwide. Any change should be made over a period of time with adequate education in advance, and with awareness of feelings. Deal with it pastorally.

Because the **sacrament of holy communion** is so precious to so many and because many have grown up being herded by ushers in a particular fashion over a long period of time, the method of administering communion and the method of getting the people forward to receive it often are sacred cows. Those ushers may have been doing it the same way for many years. Whether it is continuous communion, by table with a blessing after each table, intinction, common cup or individual glass, wine or grape juice, all these practices hold a lot of former baggage that is not easily changed or given up by the present congregation. Especially when former clergy have harangued the congregation about only one way being right, you are really tramping on the toes of those people who revered that former spiritual leader when you come in and change this immediately.

It's not nearly as easy to change the **time of worship or to add a service** as one might think. People's life routines often have been set around when they go to church and what they do before and afterward — it's part of the liturgy of their special day. It is a mistake to believe that if you have several services on a Sunday morning, you can simply offer a radical change of worship at one of them and those who do not like that will go to another. Once Christians' pattern of worship is set, they'll almost always go to the same hourly service no matter what is being done there or whether they like it or not.

The way people are ushered in and out of church is another important issue to folks who are not yet able to see the larger picture of worship and worship space. Often the people who do the ushering are older and sometimes may not even be particularly religious people. There's usually a small group who never quite make it to worship, in fact, and spend the time they are not ushering in the narthex or lobby talking to each other and kibitzing about a lot of things other than God's presence with them. Be careful about handing down new methods that you expect the ushers to follow. It's important to win the ushers to your side and point out to them some problems or opportunities and let them help come up with a new method of handling them.

Older organized Sunday school classes who have their own area in the church building can be especially intransigent sacred cows. Often they have paid for the furnishings in that little space which they have now staked out as their turf into which no one else is to enter. That space sometimes represents older teachers of the class who taught it for 40 years and insisted that it always remain there. In order to be faithful to that teacher's memory, it's so important to the class that everything remain the same in that space, often because of the constant threat of change throughout the rest of their daily lives.

Adult choirs build traditions rapidly and cling to them tenaciously. Certainly they can be sacrosanct in the parish as well as all the others listed in this chapter. Because choirs give so much of their life to the church and they're on the inside of the planning and carrying out of the worship, they become very close to each other. As church choirs often attract very loyal members, they do have strong traditions that they want followed in order not to upset or challenge their role in the worship experience.

If you are a pastor in a congregational building that has **an altar,** that altar represents God's presence in a special way and is a very sacred cow as to where it's located. While it would seem so easy simply to move an altar out from the wall, remember that the altar represents God's presence at Uncle Joe's funeral, daughter Mary's wedding and the first communion of Sarah and Billy. In addition, if it's a more liturgical worship service, children have served there as acolytes, and volunteers have served as assisting ministers and lectors. There have probably been some clergy in the past who have taught confirmation classes and convinced those young minds that there's just one place for an altar and that the pastor faces the congregation sometimes and faces the altar other times. Because they revered this former pastor, to move the altar is to upset all those symbolic memories and religious feelings of days gone by.

One of the most special people in many parishes is the **former retired pastor** who still remains there. An interesting thing about time is that it often cleans up the criticisms and imperfections of a former pastor who becomes much more holy after leaving the leadership position of that parish! The **widow of the former pastor** is in the same category. Because of the phenomenon of more and more of our clergy owning their own homes, it has increasingly encouraged the policy for the retired pastor to stay right in the congregation. While I don't believe that's a good practice, we must learn how to deal with this reality, demonstrating the proper respect the clergy should have and the transference of pastoral authority from him or her to us. This means, of course, that each time retired clergy are in attendance at any event, we recognize them. We, as the new clergy, ought to immediately recommend their status as a pastor emeritus, and often visit them, asking their advice and counsel. Pay attention to their spouse, as well. Just remember that these people are often dearly loved and unreasonably revered, and we must treat them with respect as the sacred images they are.

Pastor Susan Nachtigal writes: "The relationship with former retired pastors still 'on site' is terribly important, however. I would try to make a case for honoring and respecting while at the same time making sure not to send mixed signals to the parishioners or the former pastor. While private consultation and guidance serves the needs of both old and new, publicly there must be no question as to who is presently 'under call.'

"When a pastor first arrives at a parish with former clergy remaining, he/she needs to come to an understanding with the former as to what are agreed upon practices, boundaries and proper arenas for input. Also, for the health of the parish, I believe that both old and new need to agree only to speak well of the other in both private and public settings."

Anna-Marie Klein writes: "Know your congregation members — including family relationships (clans). No church is like any other church, but every congregation functions like a family. Not all church families are as functional as others. Much of what happens is tradition or custom, and not right or wrong. Congregations, like families, have their own pace, mode, expectations. Changes come without trauma when they happen with consensus, naturally evolve, and/or the church family makeup changes and members assume different church roles."

Not infrequently the **choir director, parish secretary, organist, custodian, or Sunday school superintendent** who has served a congregation for a long time also falls into this category. These people work as volunteers and give a lot of their life to the church. Because of their sacrificial service, they have done favors for many people in the parish who feel the congregation owes them a lot. Before retiring the people who fill this kind of role, be sure that much support and consensus is gained for doing that and that it is done with great recognition, expression of appreciation and respect.

There are **certain shut-ins** in each congregation like the former pastor or his spouse, a long-time Sunday school teacher, a choir director and community leaders and/or people who are perceived to have money and power who are sacred cows in the parish. In praise of their work on behalf of the church and their ministry in daily life in the community, immediate attention by you through visitation of them, and an overall recognition of the long service these people have given will not only be consistent with our servant ministry image, but also a wise move to gain support from your new congregants. Recognize their birthdays, anniversaries, and send them notes of appreciation.

Watch out for **things which have been given by members of the church** or by members now deceased of families still active in the church which are tools and objects aiding our worship, such as memorial candlesticks, communionware, baptismal font and chancel furniture, objects of art with little brass plaques on them designating who have given them. Even to move them within the building takes a lot of finesse and support by members of the family who have an investment in them and/or other folks who are simply used to seeing them in that place and used in that fashion for a long time.

Pastor William Wong adds to this chapter this sage advice: "Some other sacred cows are worship liturgy, festivals, annual activities like the St. Lucia festival, rummage sales, etc. Dealing with the comment, 'We've always done it this way,' will not be easy. Change should be introduced carefully, compassionately, slowly and pastorally. It can lead to conflict, so be careful."

Pastor Winkel is concise on the subject of sacred cows: "Recognize their existence, take your time, make them allies, involve key players in decision-making, and celebrate their meaning and how they will become more meaningful in new settings and configurations."

These sacred cows, which may be objects, people or customs, can be instruments through which God's spirit enables us to be more effective in our pastoral ministry or they can be obstacles which can trip us up and set us back in our mission to be faithful clergy and lead the congregation in their worship and witness. Often a pastoral relations committee or a mutual ministry committee or even the call committee that brought us to the parish can be helpful in identifying these things which are overly precious to the congregation and to which we should pay special attention and care. A former clergy person or long-time member can also be helpful in their identification.

Establishing And
Maintaining Boundaries

While flying from Dayton, Ohio, to Oakland, California, on American flight #459, after preaching at my alma mater, Wittenberg University in Springfield, I prepared for my class on "Evangelism, Stewardship and Ministry." In particular, I worked on a lecture which I sensed very much needed to be shared on the topic of establishing and maintaining boundaries as a parish pastor.

After giving this lecture in my class, Dr. Eldon Olson, Region 1 counselor to pastors, helped me sharpen its focus and add several points, included here. Reading required for discussion of this subject in class (and highly recommended by me) are the books *Is Nothing Sacred?* by Marie Fortune and *Sex in the Forbidden Zone,* by Peter Rutter, M.D. After observing during my 29 years' parish ministry the traps and temptations in the area of sexual abuse by the pastor, I believe the following list of suggestions will help prevent such temptation and abuse:

1. **Dress in a more formal fashion.** Clergy can continually remind parishioners of the holy office they fill and remind themselves at the same time.

2. **Avoid long-term counseling.** This is one of the most important ways for clergy to protect themselves and to maintain boundaries. Pastor Kelly Denton-Borhaug adds: "If someone needs help beyond two to three sessions, I try to refer." Not only does long-term counseling sap time away from other ministries — and sometimes prevents the counselee from getting the most professional help — but it can also lead to an inappropriate level of intimacy between pastor and parishioner.

3. **Have a third party nearby.** In any counseling setting it is important for a third party to be close by. Often you can keep a study door ajar. Wise church secretaries have learned

to monitor counseling sessions with great discretion. They may be trained to interrupt if the session gets too long.

4. **When possible, include the counselee's family in the counseling.** Including members of a counselee's family not only makes for more effective counseling, it also ensures that appropriate boundaries between pastor and parishioner are maintained.

5. **Be aware of whose needs you are fulfilling.** Ask yourself if you are fulfilling your needs or the parishioner's when ministering closely with another person. Sometimes our own ego needs, desire for power or other human need can lead to a deterioration of boundaries.

6. **Use discretion with home visits.** Clergy need to be aware of the vulnerability inherent at times when visiting someone alone at home. Sometimes you can take someone else with you or you can meet someone at a restaurant. Make an appointment and stay no longer than 30 minutes. Keep on or about your person symbols of a professional visit.

7. **Ask parishioners to address you as "Pastor."** This small formality reminds clergy and their parishioners of the holy office held by the pastor. A "Pastor Jerry" or "Pastor Mary" may provide just the right balance between formality and informality.

8. **Respect another person's space.** Clergy should always be cautious of inappropriate body contact, such as brushing up against someone, or prolonging hugging to the point that it becomes sensuous (or might be interpreted as such). A hug is not to be a mad embrace.

9. **Choose language meticulously.** Be aware of language that might be construed as sexually inviting. This means avoiding use of sexual innuendo, and being very cautious about using expressions of endearment which might be misinterpreted.

10. **Be careful when traveling.** When traveling to meetings, synod assemblies, and so forth with other church members, clergy should conduct themselves in the most professional manner to avoid vulnerability to and charges of impropriety.

11. **Form a pastoral relations committee.** This group can be one of the greatest helps to the pastor and the congregation, to be consulted by both over any questionable practices.
12. **Avoid work situations that may lead to vulnerability or speculation.** While working closely with employees is beneficial to "getting the job done," it is important to use discretion in work situations that might put you or the employee in a vulnerable position or cause speculation by others. Be aware of "how things look." Two cars parked alone in the parking lot at night can be just enough grist for the rumor mill!
13. **Be cautious in counseling when divorce is involved.** Clergy need to do their best to remain impartial when a couple is seeking a divorce in order to avoid accusations of favoritism or inappropriate involvement with either one of the couple. Do couple counseling with both members present.
14. **Trust your spouse's intuition.** A pastor's spouse can be quick to pick up on another's attraction to the pastor. This intuition can be very valuable!
15. **Be aware of times of extreme vulnerability.** Clergy need to understand how vulnerable people are particularly after they've experienced a loss through death or divorce. Beware of your own times of fatigue, loneliness, or spiritual emptiness.
16. **Avoid drinking in excess.** In any setting, clergy need to be mindful of drinking to the point that self-discipline in language or action is lost. Better not to drink at all while in the pastoral role. Be careful about showing up at any function with alcohol on your breath. Pastor Robert Winkel adds: "Don't get in the habit of using drink to reward or relax yourself after a demanding parish schedule or Sunday worship."
17. **Practice prudence in developing intimate friendships.** Clergy need to go slowly, and even practice restraint, as they establish friendships, especially when they begin a new ministry. Forming intimate friendships right off the bat, before really getting to know someone, can eventually lead to problems. Best friends may need to be found outside of your parish.
18. **If you are married, endeavor to keep your own marriage relationship healthy.** While a healthy marriage will not

always deter sexual abuse, it will make it less likely to occur. Maintain the boundaries between marriage and your professional life.

19. **Keep rested, find relief from stress and remain spiritually fit.** This is perhaps the most important suggestion for all clergy and the most effective way to avoid unpastoral behavior!

20. **Maintain a referral list of personally selected professional resources.** These might be qualified counselors, lawyers or treatment specialists. Know their expertise and competencies.

21. **Develop a relationship with a supervising counselor.** A peer group might fill this role if you are in a remote area.

22. **Do not provide counseling in certain situations.** Serve only as a referral agent in the following six situations which require professional counseling: chemical or alcohol abuse, domestic violence, anger management, victims of childhood sexual abuse, eating disorders, or legal/financial matters.

Pastor Denton-Borhaug adds: "Women clergy especially should expect to be sought out by victims of clergy sexual abuse and other kinds of sexual abuse. I have been astonished at how this abounds! Get educated as to these realities and be ready to listen and refer. Also know your denomination's policy regarding misconduct of clergy."

The Reverend Dr. Don Hillerich of Sarasota, Florida, advises: "Maintain a professional atmosphere with chairs separated, a desk or table between, and have lots of family pictures to send a proper message."

Trying in earnest to follow every one of the above suggestions, and being ever mindful of the least appearance of impropriety, would probably a very paranoid pastor make, not to mention an ineffective one! However, the present epidemic of sexual improprieties and abuse by clergy mandates that you consider all of these suggestions carefully. As clergy begin or continue their ministries, they'll find that the boundaries they establish and maintain will be deeply appreciated by all of the congregation.

The Pastor's Personal Stewardship

As one of God's servants called to ministry living in our culture, we need carefully think through what we believe and live out as God's caretakers of all creation. In the Genesis account we learn that God created all that exists and it is good — and we are in charge for a while. So we are called to be stewards of all God's creation in a living, nurturing, preserving way. Consider the implications.

Let's look first at the stewardship of our own money. It certainly is very important that we keep good financial records. In a day of taxes, loopholes, sheltered annuities, and tax filing by computer, it is important to have carefully planned and worked out a method of recording what we receive and how we spend it. This record also gives us a good guard against wealth addiction and an opportunity to see the overall picture of the accumulation and distribution of our wealth.

Our own personal stewardship means that we must keep a reasonableness in our use of credit cards. With interest rates often between 12% and 15% on the unpaid balance each month, it simply is not good stewardship to keep a balance that we must pay on and to overuse the credit available on our credit card. If we need to borrow money, better stewardship is practiced by obtaining a different kind of loan than using the credit card for that reason.

In order to make sure our priorities remain correct as one of God's called people to parish ministry and also set an example for the congregation, we must tithe of our own income. I believe tithing ought to be the minimum starting place and that we can continue to increase the proportion of our income we give away throughout the remainder of our life. I also think it is very beneficial for us to share with our congregation these practices of our financial stewardship. It certainly is consistent with being an example to others and living the exemplary life that we promised to do in our ordination vows.

Certainly, wise use of savings accounts and investment opportunities is good financial stewardship. Some checking accounts pay interest and some don't. Some savings book accounts are quite small in interest compared with what we might do in other methods of investing. There's nothing irreligious about shopping for the best interest from our investments.

Certainly the pastor wants to teach and set an example for good money management in his or her family. There aren't many places where children get this kind of counsel and example. We who are clergy can set that example by the way we do it and how open we are in sharing our methods with our family.

While I think other causes ought to be kept at a minimum compared with the Body of Christ, we need to think out very carefully the other causes that we support in addition to our church. I believe that we communicate something when we contribute to such institutions as our seminary, church-related college, Amnesty International, and other causes in which we believe deeply.

As good financial stewards we will certainly want to give to institutional organizations of the church outside the local congregation to demonstrate and live out what we say, when we put forth the idea of the global church. Because few seminary alumni have much money, every alum ought to support his or her seminary in a strong and loyal fashion.

It's my practice to support only altruistic organizations which follow good stewardship themselves. Sometimes as much as 50-70% of your donation to an organization will be used in overhead and not get to the people it is organized to help. A pastor, as a good steward, will know these percentages and select carefully where to give money.

We should have a good estate plan in place no matter what our age. Pastor Hillerich comments: "See an estate planner, pay the fee, do it right." This means a will is made out which designates the Body of Christ as one of the chief recipients of whatever our estate is when we die. Memorials and bequests are certainly ways of witnessing.

In addition to financial management, I hasten to go further with you and talk about other perhaps even more important considerations for the pastor as a personal steward. Our bodies and physical health are gifts and we need to care for them very well. Also a part of this gift is our mental health and we need to live a lifestyle which keeps it healthy. This certainly means that we must be good managers of our time and energy, not abusing our body emotionally or physically. It impacts on what we eat or don't eat and certainly includes wise shopping in the supermarket.

Identifying our God-given gifts shows a good sense of stewardship to our congregants and to ourselves by finding ways of determining how God has especially blessed us. We then determine ways of using these special gifts in our daily ministry in order to benefit the development of God's mission and ministry through us. Counseling centers and professional guidance organizations can help us determine just what we ought to capitalize on because God has blessed us so richly in that area.

Pastor Nachtigal writes: "Identifying our own personal gifts reflects a good sense of stewardship benefiting both our congregation and ourselves. When we determine how God has especially blessed us with particular characteristics and a particular personality, then we can determine ways of using these special gifts in our daily ministry to further God's mission and ministry."

A good steward will want to have a living will made out and his or her family members agree to it and know about it. He or she may also want to have a designation for donation of his or her organs at the time of sudden death. What a beautiful opportunity to be a steward of our physical body for maintaining life and giving new life to others who require transplantation.

For a pastor to live the steward's lifestyle means that we must be able to discern between those things which are luxuries and those things which are necessities. We cannot depend on the people who live around us as they often gather their creature comforts and then worry about protecting them. Nor can we go along with most media advertising as to what's necessary for the good quality of life. Think carefully about creature comforts like having more than one television set, boats, campers, club memberships, which might seem very important but actually are superficial in the enrichment of our lives.

We should avoid fads in such things as clothing, entertainment, movements and causes, and toys for adults. It's easy to get sucked up into the latest craze and invest ourselves and our money in it only to find that it is much less than permanent and of little significance to life itself.

The wise use of cars and the way we transport ourselves needs to be examined if we're going to be a good pastor steward. The model of our car and the amount of energy it consumes in transporting us is no longer a pious option as we think about the limited natural resources of God's created earth.

Even the way we heat and cool our homes is an ethical question. Energy audits and sensitivity to the use and misuse of resources necessary to keep us comfortable is an issue of real significance to the real steward.

How we treat non-human life in our world ought to be examined. The natural resources, the rich earth itself, which produced food, the pollution of the ecosystem all are spiritual and theological considerations that the pastor steward will want to examine carefully and set the example for others.

Our witness in the pulpit about our personal lifestyle decisions as a steward will be deeply appreciated by our congregation. We need not present it as if we know all the answers but simply communicate that it is very important to all God's people to take seriously being good managers of all that God has given us so that those born after us might have the privilege of resource inheritance that we have taken for granted. There are certain basic mistakes that can be made in our stewardship of money:

1. Giving off the bottom of our income rather than the top is a mistake. So often we adopt a certain lifestyle, pay for it, and then give to the church some of what is left.

2. Deciding to give or not to give, based on whether we like what's happening at the congregational level. We usually tell our congregants that this is a mistake they shouldn't make partly because we have invested in their giving. However, this ought to be true of the leadership of the congregation as well. We give to God, not to any one congregation.

3. Arriving at the size of our offering by comparing what others give or by what's respectable as a member of that congregation. The proportion of what we have is what we ought to consider prayerfully. The amount we give ought to have some relationship to our theology which states that God owns it all anyway and simply loans some of it to us to use for a while.

4. Giving only to support a cause rather than as a response to all that God has done for us. There are a lot of good causes we could give to, feeling God would applaud. However, our need to give is a lot stronger than any organization's need to have what we contribute. Giving away a large portion of what we receive keeps our priorities in order and maintains our sanity as one of God's disciples. In the world we live in and our culture here in the United States, we simply must give large portions in order to resist the wealth addiction that is so seductive and on all sides of us.

We don't give as if paying dues to other organizations. We don't give for services rendered. We give because it is a wonderful response to what God has already done for us.

One of the real joys of being a pastor is that we can think through our own stewardship and that we have the challenging ministry of helping others with theirs. In our regular, year round preaching on the subject, we can find instruction for ourselves as well.

The Team Ministry

After many years as a senior pastor serving together with associates, assistants and associates in ministry, I offer the following suggestions.

The most helpful book I have found on the subject of team ministry is Lyle Schaller's *Multiple Staff and the Larger Church* (Abingdon Press, 1980). While not always appreciated, Schaller's concept of the senior pastor being the "tribal chief" and the "number one medicine man" needs to be well understood in order to make a team ministry work and to understand the dynamics in most larger congregations with staff ministry.

It is very important that each pastor on the staff has his/her own support group. It does not work to use one pastoral relations committee or mutual ministry committee for two or more pastors. Select from the congregation a small group of people to be your sounding board and help you work through the muddy waters of who's in charge and what your part of the ministry should be and really is. The Reverend David Ullery of Worthington, Ohio, adds: "... but the chairs of the committees should relate, and insure consistency or each committee could work to protect 'their' pastor."

One of the most difficult things for associate pastors to understand is that an important element of their ministry is to work hard for the congregation to respect and follow the guidance of the senior pastor. There needs to be an intentionality on the associate pastor's part to make the senior pastor look good. This is an idea that is often fought by many associate pastors, especially those who have difficulty working in a pastoral team. There must be a trusted loyalty to each other. What it really means is that the associate pastor will be aware of the senior pastor's weak points and help compensate for them so that the senior pastor continues to be effective and also be perceived as a good leader for the congregation.

The Reverend Dr. Robert Hock, a longtime senior pastor in Winter Park, Florida, takes a little different point of view: "I think of 'team ministry' as each team member enabling each other to 'shine' and not serve — not just the senior pastor."

When setting out the tasks that each will do, it's important that each pastor has some of the "winners" and some of the "losers" in parish programs. Perhaps the terms "visible" and "invisible" would better explain the concept. There are some ministries like caring for the young single adults that rarely bring a good payoff in the eyes of the congregation. There are other ministries that are almost always attractive and look successful to the people of God. Each pastor needs to have some of each.

It's also important to let it be known that the other clergy person speaks for you. It is crucial that the senior pastor back up whatever the associate pastor says, no matter how badly they disagree with the comments. If an associate pastor can be confident that the senior pastor will operate in this mode, it gives the associate a sense of self-worth and well-being that enables him or her to carry out a full ministry, too.

Be aware of the mentality that many congregations have in assuming the role of an assistant pastor is not altogether a full ministry and that all associates are working toward someday being a senior pastor, or "someday he'll/she'll get their own parish." It needs to be made perfectly clear that being an associate or assistant is a full career, and a specialty in itself. In fact, it's my conviction that it takes more skill, humility, self-esteem and maturity to be an assistant or associate than it does to be senior pastor! This is especially true if the assistant or associate is working well and making the team ministry look good.

It's important to avoid trying to be like the other pastor on the team. Celebrate your own differences and don't insist on the same work habits or lifestyle of your partner in ministry. We all work differently and ought to find the humor in that. While one effective pastor may have a very messy desk and study, the other might be meticulously clean and well

45

organized. If the two can learn to live with each other it will probably make for a fairly good pastoral team. Pastor Wong writes: "You need the commitment by all the staff to work as a team. It's like a marriage: you must work at it."

Preventing Trouble

It's important, at the outset of a new ministry, that there be carefully worked out job descriptions for each staff person, especially for the senior pastor and associates. Equally important is carrying out annual evaluations by a pastoral relations committee and between the pastoral team, based on these job descriptions. The descriptions will need to be updated and modified annually with opportunity for the associate pastor to take on new or needed areas. An employee handbook with as much as possible spelled out helps.

It is also important that there be agreement on what happens when the senior pastor leaves the pastorate. In fact, if this is not covered by the constitution or by-laws, there should be a letter of agreement written into the call and signed by all parties so that everyone is clear on how that will work.

Be absolutely sure that the congregation understands who is responsible for what and publish that list frequently.

At least once a year, meet as a pastoral team and set your long-term and short-term goals together and agree on them. It helps immensely if each understands the other's top priorities and expectations and why they place the emphasis they do on their ministries.

On The Job

Being on a pastoral team calls for very intentional communication. Notes and memos are helpful, but won't do by themselves. There needs to be at least one meeting a week when all concerns are shared. This meeting must be conducted with integrity and frankness for the benefit of those in attendance. If you're feeling hostility or jealousy toward the other person, those *feelings* as well as you *think*, must be shared honestly

46

so they can be out in the open and dealt with in a professional manner.

It is important that an associate pastor with a criticism go to the senior pastor and have it out honestly and in private when the disagreements come. Just don't make the criticism of your teammate in public!

One of the highest skills needed by an associate and senior pastor is an ability to handle criticism by members of the congregation of the other pastor in a professional fashion. It's tempting to have your own ego pumped by these criticisms, but crucial that you don't let people get between you and the other pastor. Do not allow yourself to be triangulated into conflicts between a pastor and a member.

Schaller's book helps you understand the need for the senior pastor, as "chief medicine man," to preside, to "work the tables" at social events, to preach more frequently and to show up at some death calls, even if the associate has already been there and taken care of it. Whatever you do, don't let any employee go around the senior pastor to you. Let your support for the senior pastor be known right away when you begin your ministry and stick by it no matter what.

They are a wise senior pastor and associate who share presiding at worship services together at least at first. Later, when you are both well established and when the relationship is much more mature, you can look at ways to cut down on duplication and save energy by not having both attend everything that goes on in the parish.

Be sure to attend conferences together that the churchwide expression provides on team ministry and other subjects. It is very helpful to do continuing education together, as that almost always provides time for good communication. Pastor Hillerich adds: "Together, discuss specific areas of learning opportunities that could benefit one another."

Do refrain from souring your spouse or kids on the other pastor. Even when you are very disappointed in that pastor's behavior, it is important not to share it with the children, as it gives them a poor image of pastoral ministry.

If Trouble Comes

No pastor likes to be blind sided! Be sure to warn the senior pastor and other staff if you are going to take some prophetic action that might cause controversy in the congregation or community. A cardinal rule for associates is never to make controversial public statements without the agreement of the senior pastor.

When the relationship between pastors becomes strained, go to a counselor together. Set up the system for doing that while things are going well between you. Don't let ego get in the way of contacting a synod's counselor or bringing someone in from Lutheran Social Services or a pastoral counseling center. Taking such action can make a difference in improving your relationships.

Whenever possible, "take the heat" for the senior pastor. While that's a very humble way of approaching ministry with a very servant-like attitude, it can be a great ministry for an assistant pastor to carry out in a community and congregation.

Do plan to stay. Pray for each other daily out loud and enjoy the benefits of that kind of intercessory prayer and God's ability to change your own attitude toward the other person.

Team ministry is tough to do. I know of few that are successful for very long. Probably the team ministries which have had the best chance of success and effectiveness on God's behalf are those where the associate pastor understands the motivation and ego of the senior pastor and the need for a congregation to have a "number one medicine man" and "tribal chief."

Paul wrote to his former congregation in Corinth these words: "After all who is Apollos? And who is Paul? We are simply God's servants, by whom you were led to believe. Each one of us does the work the Lord gave him to do: I planted the seed, Apollos watered the plant, but it was God who made the plant grow. The one who plants and the one who waters really do not matter. It is God who matters, for God makes the plant grow. For we are partners working together for God, and you for God's field." — 2 Corinthians 3:5-7 and 9.

Pastor As Public Minister:

Doing Ministry

Pastor As Public Minister:

Doing Ministry

Leading Worship

Now that I am a seminary president and professor, I visit about 48 congregations a year as their preacher and thus observe many different styles of worship leadership. As I am flying high over Des Moines, Iowa, on United #784 from Chicago to Oakland, I have the following thoughts about leading worship.

Be cautious about your demeanor as you lead worship. Some pastors are so comfortable in the chancel that they seem to put the entire congregation at ease, who can then perform and enjoy a worthwhile, relaxing and pleasant worship experience. Other clergy arrive in the chancel so ill at ease that it is transferred to the congregation and people leave with a sense of incompleteness and uncertainty. Even though it may be so, it ought not look as if we have just come out of a very frantic church school hour, adult forum, committee meeting or counseling session. That period just before we lead worship is crucial in establishing a close connection with God's spirit and allowing that spirit to take over as we empower our people to worship and it is caught by other members of the congregation.

The single biggest criticism I have of some of the worship leadership I have seen is that the pastor fails to preside and take charge. There seems to be an uncertainty about the presiding role in the first place and the pastor's authority to undertake it in the second, which the congregation senses and which makes them uneasy. That presence, which communicates by tone of voice, eye contact, sincerity of personality and enthusiasm for the task, is extremely important in leading worship. We want to be reverent but not rigid. While we don't want to appear arrogant in the chancel, we do want to put people at ease by conveying a sense of self-confidence, and that comes from knowing we are in charge and well prepared.

I have been in a number of congregations where lay ministry was interpreted narrowly to mean that we put albs on lay people and have them help in the worship service. The worship in the chancel becomes like a three-ring circus, and the clergy nearly get lost as people come and go, voice levels and volumes change dramatically from one person to another, and people almost step on each other as they come forward for their part of the liturgy. One or two assisting ministers is enough! Let that person (or persons) be well prepared and let the two or three of you do the worship in a deeply spiritual and well rehearsed method. Try to avoid the appearance of a stage manager with people entering and exiting stage right and stage left.

At the seminary, I often see new worship leaders mouth the directions for the congregation, but never really put voice to them. I think this is a mistake. When we are self-confident and in charge, we need to give the worship directions out loud if we're going to mouth them at all. Another related mistake is to allow the ends of our sentences to trail off, assuming people know what we're meaning to say. Even better may be to put needed directions in an easily understood bulletin.

Because there are currently two versions of The Lord's Prayer in use and printed in many worship books, do lead out in a strong voice the first petition worded in the language of whichever version you want used. If you leave this up to most of the congregation, many will use one version (the older one) while others will use the newer, international version. In some congregations they will even try to be the loudest with their preferred version in order to get everyone to do it their way. Take charge, lead out, give direction, especially in that first petition!

A number of times I am distracted by all sorts of combinations of words in such simple things as announcing the scripture for the day. Why not simply use the directions out of the worship book and announce it in a very definite and specific fashion teach time? Try not to say that the lesson is "found" in a certain chapter! Avoid announcing the gospel by calling it a gospel lesson. And avoid ending the reading by saying,

"Here ends the Gospel for the day." (Hopefully the remainder of the service will also contain gospel!) Attention to these details will make a much cleaner use of language throughout the liturgy. Do try to avoid a "holy tone" whereby the liturgy and scripture is preached in a preachy fashion rather than announced as a herald would announce it. Someone has called this the "stained glass voice syndrome," and while it might be a notch above a monotone worship leader, it is not much of a notch above! You ought to be able to use good lecture recital and oral interpretation of literature methodology as we speak in our worship services.

Be sure that gestures and other body language suggest the same message as verbal communication. It's always odd to me to see someone with a broad, sweet smile on his or her face while at the same time talking about a very grim reality. The opposite is even more dramatic: because of fear of being where we are, we develop somewhat of a stone face that is expressionless and does not reflect the humor, playfulness, terror, or awesomeness of that which is said and read.

We need to understand our orientation and movement in the chancel. This has changed dramatically over the years with changes in some denomination's worship manuals and with moving the altar away from the wall by still others. Nevertheless, it's good to have in mind whether the words we are saying are *speaking to God's people* or *speaking on behalf of God's people to God.* Some call this the sacramental and sacrificial elements of worship. It simply means that when we have prayer, we pray it, and when we speak to the people, we address the people. Our altar prayers can become the oddest combination of all these elements mixed together and the average worshiper isn't sure who is being addressed or on whose behalf the leader is speaking.

Good communication of the gospel and proclamation of the good news from the chancel and pulpit means that we have excellent eye contact. If you have ever been told that the way to overcome your fright of addressing people is to look over their heads or to imagine that they are all seated there naked, forget that advice! It is so tempting to avoid the eyes of worshipers and not focus on anyone. This does not make for good communication. Looking into the eyes of a person and for a little bit, and then moving on to another person, is good technique. It will also draw out of us more effective communication than we had even planned to give.

Even though we may be excellent speakers, old habits do return time and time again. Everyone needs a critic to remind them of what they are doing when they lead worship and preach. Word whiskers and vocalized pauses are the worst offenses and can be annoying to worshipers to the extent of absolutely ruining their worship experience. Try to get rid of "you knows" and "uhs" in your language when trying to think of the next thing to say.

It is interesting to me that in the last few years we have paid so little attention to the art of gestures. Our hand movements can be winsome, attractive and aid our liturgical movements, or they can be rough, hostile and work against good liturgy and preaching. I notice that so many clergy, when they are trying to seat the congregation, will put their palms forward and make a gesture which looks like they are pushing the congregant down in the pew. A much better gesture is to extend the hands outward and palms up as if you are letting the person down into the pew. Check your gestures and see if they are communicating what your real feelings are toward your congregation and your position as worship leader.

Watch out, too, for how much you're holding in your hands as you conduct worship. The very finest worship leader will memorize the liturgy and not be encumbered by books, pamphlets, paper clips, book markers, bulletins, and so forth, that are often held in plain view of the congregation. Take time ahead of the worship service to get so organized that even if you read the worship liturgy, you have places marked and printed material placed in such a way that you are not juggling all this stuff in front of your congregation as you try to lead worship.

Pastor Denton-Borhaug writes: "Marty Haugen speaks of the importance of 'swallowing the books' so that as we have

54

worship we are really present with the community and not still in a book. I try to memorize as much of the liturgy as I can."

The Reverend William Wong adds: "Learn to project your voice. Speak with enough force to fill the room. Learn to use microphones and be comfortable with them. Speak with confidence and pronounce words clearly. Microphones do not clean up poorly enunciated words. People with poor hearing will appreciate your efforts. Mistakes will happen. It's okay. Don't let it fluster you. Either go on or acknowledge it and then go on. A good laugh may be appropriate in this situation."

All these items are common sense things that can either enhance or distract as we serve in a very special way as God's ambassadors in leading God's people to worship the Almighty.

Conducting Weddings

Good pre-marital counseling is increasingly more difficult to require. However, try your best to get from four to six sessions before the actual wedding takes place. A session or two of planning the wedding with parents of bride and groom, as well, will serve to build a rapport and see that the wedding is done well.

Sometimes those people who simply want to be married at their home, in their back yard, in the church parsonage or in the pastor's office can be convinced to attend a worship service of the congregation and be married within the context of that worship service. I found the Saturday night service just splendid for that opportunity. I called the couple forward after the offering, married them, and then had the congregational members greet them after the service. Everybody loved it. Because we are pastors of a congregation we probably do our best work marrying people in that most familiar context of the church building. Pastor Wong states: "The wedding service is a worship service. It is more than just the celebration of the uniting of two people. God is a major focus of this celebration."

Pastor Nachtigal adds: "When a wedding is at a church one has the opportunity to 'fill out' the service ... the opportunity to use music and readings and candles and to give the service substance. I think that couples should be encouraged to, within a liturgical context, mold their service (with the pastor's help) into something that expresses their praise and love of God, along with their love for one another. (Even **with** all of this the service is barely a half hour.) I very much discourage 'quick' wedding ceremonies."

There are evangelism opportunities in the extended congregation for weddings we conduct even when neither bride nor groom is a member. I encourage you to take most weddings you are encouraged to do. Find the unchurched; relate to them and see the wedding not only as a service to them, but also as an outreach opportunity. Pastor Hillerich is probably correct when he claims that "a very small percentage will become active; but, we should still do it."

If your congregation does more than five or six weddings a year, have a volunteer wedding coordinator. This person can take much of the burden from organizing and actually running the wedding the day of the service, relating to the bride and groom, and handling those minutia that a florist would do if you allow them that latitude during the service itself. A wedding coordinator can remove a lot of the little worries about the mechanics of the rehearsal and wedding.

Try to convince your congregation that it is less appropriate to conduct weddings during Lent. If one must be held during that season, educate them to the fact that flowers, lots of candles, and celebratory music are just not appropriate for that season of the year. This, in itself, will often discourage Lenten weddings.

Schedule the rehearsal so it comes before the rehearsal dinner. Keep it early enough in the evening that you can still have the evening for yourself and your family, if necessary. Most rehearsals can be done in a half hour to 45 minutes. Begin with a prayer, introduce yourself, have everybody seated in the first couple of rows of the sanctuary, talk the participants through the wedding, walk them through without the music and then do it with the music. Save the actual words of the service for the wedding day.

As you instruct the ushers at the rehearsal, try to convince everyone concerned that rarely do we divide up the congregation into the bride's side and the groom's side. This often can be embarrassing and certainly is not inclusive in nature. During the introduction be sure to warn them about how drinking can ruin the wedding and formally let them know that you will not tolerate drunken participants at the service.

Attend the rehearsal dinner if possible, and bring your spouse along. Remember that they'll often ask you what is expected at a rehearsal dinner. These can be very awkward times. Offering a toast to the bride and groom and their parents will be seen as your expression of love and desire for friendship with them.

In wedding planning watch out for any kind of encouragement of ring bearers or flower girls in the service under the age of five or six who can distract and ruin a wedding. If they insist, be sure to help them develop options, such as seating the child after the processional.

You, the bride and groom, and the parents will have to determine if the majority of the people who will be attending are what you would think of as "church people." This will determine how much you want to use the liturgy in your denominational service book and whether you want to sing hymns and so forth. It will also be a big factor in whether you want to offer Holy Communion as a part of the service. Sometimes it is appropriate and sometimes not. Be very sensitive to the fact that some of the people in the wedding party may not be church people at all and thus would be very embarrassed if communion was offered and it was obvious to the congregation that they did not take it. Wear your appropriate vestments. Remember that the color of the paraments remains for the church year and is not changed for a wedding. If you will take time to prepare a guidelines booklet for weddings at your church, it will help the couple do their planning.

If at all possible, convince the bride and groom that music like "Here Comes the Bride" is just not appropriate and rarely used anymore. Other more churchly pieces will show much better liturgical and musical taste.

Be careful about exclusiveness, and also sexism, in the wedding. See if you can convince the parents of the bride and groom to escort their son and daughter forward. It just isn't very appropriate anymore to have the father of the bride give her away. It's never appropriate to have the father of the bride give her away when it is not a first wedding. Pastor Denton-Borhaug says she encourages a public blessing and affirmation for the couple from both sets of parents.

The procession down the aisle to the chancel looks best now if it is done by couples, rather than by the bridesmaids filing down by themselves.

Remember that the bride and groom probably won't remember or even hear most of the homily that you give. Be sure to include the congregation who are more likely to hear it. This is an opportunity to witness to the sacredness of marriage and the help that our theology and church can provide in keeping that marriage and commitment of fidelity life long.

Don't get caught up in deciding in what order people should stand in the reception line! You can't win on that one. If you have a wedding coordinator, that person ought to be up to snuff on receiving lines. If you don't have a coordinator, warn the bride and groom ahead of time that they will need to work that out before the rehearsal. Pastor Ullery advises, "reception lines are becoming passé. Frequently the bride/groom release people from the church."

By all means, go to the reception and celebrate with the family. Wear your collar, have a drink, dance, circulate and "work the tables" getting acquainted. If there is a meal, often you'll be called upon for a prayer to begin in.

A few weeks later, visit the unchurched in the wedding party and do follow-up inviting them to be a part of the congregation.

Photography and video are very much a part of a wedding. Meet those who will photograph and lay out your rules of conduct for them before the wedding.

It takes a very wise diplomat to conduct a parish wedding. You are dealing with years of accumulated emotional memories that blend with fantasy in the growing up years. Deal with family members gently, but firmly, and assert in a humble way that you are in charge. And while it seems like it is the bride's wedding, in effect it is the church's wedding for the groom and bride and the families of both.

Conducting Funerals

I have the following suggestions concerning the conduct of funerals in your parish. It pays to honor almost all requests to do funerals, whether the deceased is related to the congregation or not. If you understand the "extended congregation" theory which informs you that most of your new members come from relatives, associates and friends of present members, you will understand why you must pay attention and minister to that "web" of the congregation who have not yet joined.

At the time of the actual grieving and funeral, it is not appropriate to lecture about funeral practices. Grieving people will almost always regress to doing things the way they have seen them or they themselves have done them before. This is reason enough to coax your congregation to make out funeral plans while they are yet living and file those with the church office. It's also a good reason to go with the family of the deceased to the funeral director's office to make the plans there with all concerned. Sometimes it's difficult to remain in charge during those days, as there will be members of the family and funeral directors and their assistants who will try hard to take over. In a firm way you must see that things are done in a dignified fashion, consistent with our theology.

Always go to the home of the deceased's family ahead of time to give comfort and encouragement and do preliminary planning for the actual service. This helps in getting better acquainted and communicates to the family that you are competent to make these arrangements for and with them.

As a pastor you'll need to be a diplomat, theologian, peacemaker, negotiator, preacher and liturgical leader as you conduct parish funerals. Keep in mind that the funeral is not primarily for the deceased, but for those still living who need the comnfort of the Gospel. Be careful that you are not proving liturgical points, but rather ministering to and loving people who mourn. It's possible to follow everything exactly as you learned it in theory in seminary, and yet offend those who have lost a loved one and to whom you are trying your best to minister. On the other hand, it's also possible to so capitulate to people who only know syrupy-civil-religion type funerals that you wind up betraying your role in the parish as prophet, priest and pastor.

Church Funerals

Because of what people have seen practiced in other churches, it's not always easy carrying out a church funeral. It is my practice always to have the casket closed during the church service and, if possible, during the entire time the casket is in the church building. The use of a funeral pall placed over the casket will help carry that out. You may have to compromise and allow viewing of the body in the back of the church until the service begins; however, once the casket is closed and is processed down the aisle to the chancel for the funeral, it should not be opened again. Try to explain this very carefully to the family and the funeral director ahead of time.

It is not easy, but we need to convince our congregants that flowers need not be transferred from the funeral home to the church, and then to the cemetery. The only flowers needed at the church are one or two arrangements which can be placed on the altar in the customary place. Remember that the color of the paraments remains consistent with the season of the year and that no special colors are used for funerals.

Before the casket is processed forward for the actual service, meet with the family in a side room and have prayer for them, that they might be comforted by that which you do in this funeral. Allow them to take their seats in the sanctuary, and then lead the casket down the aisle to the chancel area. It's customary for the casket to remain lengthwise, headfirst, at the end of the aisle, just in front of the chancel steps (except for the burial of clergy, when it should be feet first).

Your leading that casket in and out will communicate to all that this is a church and you are the pastor and you are conducting the service. Be sure to wear your proper vestments and use the funeral pall on the casket.

Pastor Nachtigal writes of her practice: "I like to begin the service with the cross and the casket at the back of the church, make the baptismal proclamation, and then enter cross, casket, family (if they wish), and last, the pastor, during the entrance hymn. The paschal candle is center front under which the casket is placed. I think this is theologically and ritually full. At the end of the service, I think it is helpful, warm and comforting for the pastor to step down next to the paschal candle and extend arm and hand over the casket for the commendation and the benediction (if there is one at that point)."

Try your best to keep control of the music selection. That's not easy. You can counsel the family who are grieving that pieces used during the funeral service may be difficult for them to sing again because of the association with this burial service.

Many denominational service books have a beautiful "Order for the Burial of the Dead" which I encourage be used. Your congregation will become familiar with it and they'll love it. Consider using a paschal candle (which is usually located at the baptismal font) placing it at the head of the casket during the service as a reminder that this is one of the baptized of God and through baptism this person has life eternal.

Try to convince the deceased's family to offer the sacrament of Holy Communion during the funeral service. The method of intinction probably works best when you have no idea how many to prepare for. You can stand at the end of the casket and have people come forward in a continuous way for intinction.

For church funerals, this order works well: if viewing is desired, suggest it take place at the funeral home. Conduct a private committal at the cemetery with just family and clergy. Gather for a memorial service at the church and a reception for the family afterwards. The more traditional order would be this: hold the viewing of the deceased at the funeral home or at the back of the church, followed by the actual funeral service in the church, a committal at the cemetery, and then return to the church for a reception for the family.

Pastor Robert Winkel says, "I have found a meaningful order in having a committal first for close family and friends and then moving to the church for a service of memorial and thanksgiving. A fellowship time following a funeral or memorials is important to enable the community to embrace the family and help with the grief and healing process."

By all means, be prepared to make suggestions and negotiate. Funeral directors want to display their services for others who'll need them one day, and much prefer to have the casket opened for this and other reasons. Be careful about putting the funeral director between your suggestions for a churchly funeral and the family's desire to do it just like they did for "good old Uncle Ted."

See that the organist and janitor are paid by the funeral director, and if the deceased is not a member of the church, see that a fee is paid for the building, if used.

Funerals In Funeral Homes

Let's look at the funeral if conducted at the funeral home. It is much more difficult for clergy to remain in control in this setting; however, you can use a printed liturgy on a leaflet that's available from the publication house and hand it out to people as they enter the funeral home. You can gently, yet firmly, let everyone know that you do not conduct funeral services any place with the casket open. Be sure to wear your portable stole, which communicates that you are the ordained conducting this service.

Greet the family and pray with them in the family room before the service begins.

If there is a request for portions of the service to be done by the Eastern Star, the Masons, or other lodges or organizations, suggest that it be done the night before in the funeral home during the visiting hours. Sometimes you can also negotiate that this be done after you have completed the committal at the cemetery. Do not allow the Christian burial service to be interrupted from when you start with the invocation until the committal is completed.

Music is much more difficult to control at the funeral home as they usually have a retired person come in to play rather sentimental stuff that many people in non-liturgical churches like.

In general, make the funeral homily short and personal. Be sure to use the name of the deceased a number of times throughout the service. Some words about the deceased and his or her life will be appreciated. Remember, you can bury those you don't know! You do know their God and the One who died for them and you need not make a judgment as to their eternal resting place.

Cremation is practiced more and more in our culture. It seems to me a wise practice to endorse, especially when transportation of the remains is a concern. If viewing is desired, that can be done first, followed by the cremation. Often, it worked well for me for the cremation to take place very soon after death and then to gather for a memorial service at the church. A few can gather with you at the cemetery either before or after the memorial service for a brief committal of the cremains if interment is desired by the family.

Try your best to avoid any kind of use of an obituary. This belongs in the newspapers. I have found it to be, however, a very meaningful experience in allowing a few members of the family to share their memories about the deceased during the funeral home service.

In planning the actual scripture, hymns, and so forth, remember that those things which are most familiar are often more meaningful when you use them at a funeral. Don't try to be profound!

Be careful not to take part in any way in horseplay or kidding which is irreverent and sometimes engaged in by the funeral director and his or her help. While they might need that relief from the constant strain of grief displayed, you are the pastor and your decorum is symbolic of a much deeper spiritual presence of God in this place.

After you've conducted the funeral in the funeral home, stay in the room with the casket and help the family take their private leave of the deceased.

Insist on leading the casket and riding in the funeral coach, which communicates that the church's pastor is the one conducting the service.

At the cemetery, lead the procession to the grave site. You can wear your portable stole right over your coat if you are in cold country. Use the order for committal in your denomination's service book.

For a committal in the cemetery following the funeral service at the church, continue to wear your vestments, in colder country adding a clergy cape and biretta. You need not remove the biretta at the cemetery.

If a military or Masonic service is demanded, after you have had the benediction following the committal, remove yourself and demonstrate visibly that your part is over, allowing them to do their ceremony at the end. (Personally, I have found the words used by Masonic lodges to be very contradictory to my theology of "saved by grace through faith.")

If you're requested to do a graveside service only, usually the order can go like this: give a greeting; read scripture; offer prayer, conduct the committal, and conclude with the benediction. Usually, that is all that will be expected, especially if you are burying an infant. Be sure the casket is closed before you begin. Sometimes a brief homily is expected in good climates when this is the only service held and it is for an older person.

Usually, as the pastor conducting the service, you are expected to take leave of a family first. Be careful about any radical promises of where the deceased might be! Usually a simple assurance that you will be praying for their comfort is just about right.

After a week or two, visit the home of the bereaved and assess how well they are doing in their "grief work."

Conversation about the deceased, the feelings of the bereaved, and the family situation now that a member is gone can all lead to beneficial counseling and prayer.

Making Hospital And Home Visits

During the first week in the parish, particularly in smaller communities, it is advisable to visit the hospital(s) in the area and make an appointment with the administrator and/or hospital chaplain. At that time become acquainted with them and learn the local procedures, making regular rounds in the hospital much easier. Usually the Council of Churches or ministerium in the community has set up certain privileges for clergy, such as a place to hang coat and hat, a chapel within the hospital confines, and those much sought after, precious parking places.

Wearing the clerical collar saves embarrassment, the need for identification, and makes it easier to get around in the hospital setting. Pastor Denton-Borhaug writes a compelling response to this opinion:

> *I want to say a word about wearing the collar. I see that you value its use very highly and encourage pastors to wear it. I have spent much time thinking about the collar and connections with pastoral ministry and authority and my own role as a clergywoman in a church that has only been ordaining women for 25 years. For me that collar is an immediate association with male ministerial authority and power. It's a symbol that I have very consciously and with much thoughtfulness chosen not to appropriate.*

> *I do not find that my authority has been diminished by my choice not to wear the collar. I appreciate the opportunities to introduce and identify myself as a clergy person; I have never had any problem visiting any part of a hospital where I needed access. Oftentimes I wear a medium-size pectoral cross; this is a symbol which I embrace and which does help to identify my role in a physical sort of way.*

I could go on about this at some length, but one final word will perhaps suffice. In San Francisco (and I suspect there are many other places where this is true as well) I have met many unchurched people who relate experiences of having been wounded by the church and who are highly suspicious of external symbols of churchly authority. I believe clergywomen as a group are more likely to hear the stories of these people than clergymen. Perhaps it feels safer to relate these stories to someone who "doesn't belong to the club" of clergymen. The collar no doubt has its positive aspect of being an immediate identifier, but I have learned that it also can have a negative impact on people.

Dress like clergy and do not arrive at bedside with hat in hand and coat still on, and a list showing calls to make, looking as if ready for a quick exit!

When making a number of calls in the same hospital, consider taking the elevator to the top floor, and then walk down between floors as you make your calls. It was an efficient way for me.

One of the first things to learn is the individual hospital system for keeping track of patients and how to identify family members in that system. Some hospitals are better at this than others. Do remember that many Christians have this time-honored game called: "Go to the hospital and see if my pastor can find me." That means one cannot rely on the hospital to identify members. An internal system in the congregation needs to be set up with several methods in place to identify hospitalized members. In addition, impress upon the people the importance of calling the church office whenever they are going into the hospital or they learn of another member going into the hospital.

I found it important to carry with me on all hospital calls my denomination's *Occasional Services* book. It made available (as usually will other non-denominational book resources) the following:

Psalms, Lessons and Prayers;

Laying on of Hands and Anointing the Sick;

Comforting the Bereaved;

Confession;

Baptism;

Commendation of the Dying; and

Celebration of Holy Communion with Those in Special Circumstances.

I also found it very symbolic to carry a small strip stole in my pocket to be used when administering the sacraments. This symbolism is quite important and meaningful to those who receive the sacrament and to those who see it administered. Private communion is appreciated. Always have a private communion kit along when making a hospital call, but do not assume everyone will want it. Ask first.

Pastor Nachtigal adds: "When giving private communion, I think it is helpful to link that experience in the hospital with the celebration of the sacrament that previous Sunday at the church, thus making the "parish family" connection. Also helpful is mentioning the oneness with the whole communion of saints in heaven and on earth. When a parish member is isolated (as in a hospital room) it seems that these 'connections' are comforting and meaningful."

In The Hospital Or Nursing Home Room

Acknowledge any other patient or visitors in the room and sense whether they should be included in prayers and conversation.

Make the visit brief. Stay focused on the purpose of the visit. Remember why you are there. (Yet, don't give the appearance of being in a hurry or being harried.) It is rarely advisable to stay all day or night with family members during a medical crisis. I believe we can even be in the way by doing so. If there are no family members or means of support available for the person, then it might be appropriate to stay longer, but consider that decision carefully, bearing in mind whose needs are really being served!

69

It is tempting, but probably not helpful to compare illnesses of your own or other patients. Beware of "free association" in your conversation, rather than a more sensitive, focused, interactive listening.

Be careful about spreading a cold or flu. This can be a real dilemma if you are not feeling well and are the only pastor. Widen the distance between you and the patient, explaining why you are doing so. Sometimes a phone call to the patient, if a phone is available to them, stating that you are not feeling well or do not want to risk passing on your cold, is deeply appreciated.

It is rarely advisable to make adjustments for the patient when requested. A more appropriate response is to offer to get the nurse to help. There is just too much risk you might interrupt the healing process or do something which works against the patient's recovery.

Use caution in what you say at the bedside of someone in a coma. If talking with family members who are present, it's better to move them outside the room and speak with them there. Never assume that the person in the coma cannot hear what is said. In these situations, it is particularly important to use very familiar words like the Lord's Prayer, or a familiar, simple hymn.

When the patient is in isolation or pre-surgery, special ministry is required. Confession, prayer or communion is almost always appropriate before surgery. When the patient cannot take anything to eat or drink by mouth, you can administer the sacrament by intinction with a portion of a wafer, which will melt when dipped in wine or moisten the lips with wine using your finger. If you tell the R.N. what you will be doing, it will relieve their anxiety also. If there is a question as to whether the patient should receive private communion, I have always determined their awareness simply by saying, for instance, "Hello, John, do you know me today?" If they knew me, I felt they had enough recognition to take part in brief confession and the sacrament. We do not give communion to those who have died or have no awareness of what they are doing. However, if it is a borderline situation, do it for the comfort of the family who watch and take part.

If the patient or family member do not wish the illness publicized, be careful about listing or even announcing their name in the prayers of the church the following week. Especially if the patient is in a mental health unit, family may find it embarrassing to have the nature of illness revealed.

It is a good idea to check the waiting room for family members if you are not able to communicate with the patient. If the patient is sleeping, I usually wake them. Nurses, aides, doctors and family members may not view your call as important enough to warrant this, but I believe it is. You will often leave patients deeply disappointed when they awaken later and discover they have missed you. I think an element of the healing process has been neglected when the pastor leaves without waking them.

Stand — rather than sit — at bedside on the side of the bed to which the patient's head is turned. This helps to be more focused and accessible to the patient, as well as a better interactive listener.

Be realistic; don't promise what may not be possible for the patient. In other words, be careful about "pie in the sky" statements of healing which imply that if faith is strong enough, wellness will come. Anna-Marie Klein writes: "Be honest with a patient. A terminally ill person knows games are being played if told they will 'get well soon.' Honesty may only be found from the pastor, providing the opportunity to minister truthfully when families deny circumstances."

In spite of some Clinical Pastoral Education supervisors' advice, I believe it is a very rare situation when you should **not** offer prayer. It is your tool. In the prayer, you can sum up the concerns you have heard in the patient's voice. It helps to communicate and make this an intimate situation if you touch the patient on the hand or forearm as you offer the prayer.

I always like to arrive at the hospital with a scripture, hymn or verse memorized, one that is full of encouragement and comfort. I almost always include it in my prayer. Many of these can be found in *Occasional Services* books of most denominations.

When in the coronary or intensive care unit, be sure to check with the nurse to gain permission to make the visit. If they know you as a mainline pastor, if you are wearing a collar, and if you come to this task in a gentle way, they will almost always arrange for you to make the visit. There is a certain amount of assertiveness and professionalism you need to emulate so that you are seen as part of the health team to those nurses and aides in charge. Pay attention to the waiting rooms of these areas as they often provide many opportunities for a ministry to take place with those who anxiously gather there.

Baptism

If the sacrament of baptism is called for in the hospital setting, tell the nurse or aide what you are planning to do. Often, they will be helpful in seeking a container and water for the sacrament. Use a portable stole and have an adult witness from the congregation present, if possible. This can be very meaningful for youth or older, retired adults to take part in on behalf of the congregation.

Explain to other patients in the room what's being done and what they are expected to do, if only to watch. If unsure of whether someone has been baptized or not, simply announce that this baptism is "in case this person has not been baptized."

It is important to dispose of the baptismal water in a reverent fashion, as it becomes a visual symbol to the patient, the health care team, and any others present. Report the act at the next worship service of the congregation, record it in the parish records, and include it in the prayer of the church at the next worship service.

When Someone Dies

Go! No matter what time of day or night, go! If it is in the middle of the night, you'll usually have to use the emergency room entrance to the hospital. (This is something to ask about when meeting with the chaplain and administrator upon arrival in the community.)

Most denominations have a "Commendation of the Dying" service in their *Occasional Services* book. Be sure to wear your stole. This symbolizes your office and the importance of what you are doing. A lot of verbiage is not called for. Just be there with the family as they take leave of the deceased. Don't forget to pray! Be very considerate of other people in the hospital and gently try to move the family out of the way of hospital personnel to a chapel or private waiting room.

The survivors of the deceased will often want to know what to do next. You can encourage them to decide on a funeral director to call and let them know that you will plan to visit with them later to work out the funeral arrangements. Be very cautious about recommending a funeral director. Give them various choices and then let them decide. The nurse will often make the actual call.

It is helpful to inform the family members that they can begin gathering information for an obituary for the paper and can begin notifying friends and relatives of the death (which is much easier done if the place and time of the funeral have been set). Friends or relatives can help survivors locate and prepare some clothing in which the deceased will be dressed if viewing is carried out. They can work on designating a memorial fund. Note that most newspapers will not print "in lieu of flowers." In some areas only the funeral directors can put obituaries into the local paper.

I found that I could be of real help if I offered to meet with the family while they met with the funeral director and made the funeral arrangements. This is especially helpful if there is only one surviving relative. Make the offer before leaving the hospital. My experience is that most funeral directors do not encourage this and that you will not be enthusiastically received at these meetings by them.

Often there will be a special person or two that you, as pastor, can notify of the death, or help a family member notify.

73

This might be a son or daughter or parent who will value your presence when finding out about the death.

After The Hospital Visit

It helps to leave evidence that you have been at the hospital if you suspect in any way that the patient would not remember. This can be a printed bulletin from last Sunday's service, your business card, or a piece of devotional material. These simple indications that you are caring for this person will also be very important to family members.

Occasionally, you will call on a person you thought was your member, but who is actually a member of another congregation. It is good practice and shows a sense of the larger church and ministry to notify that person's pastor (as long as you have the patient's permission) as soon as possible.

I always liked to keep a list on my desk of those people in the hospital and pray for them by name each morning during my devotions. My membership always knew that I was doing this and I believe they felt a certain strength and love from it. I surely did. Some larger church offices keep an up-to-date chalkboard list in the lobby of all members in the hospital.

A Home Visit

The following are some steps to consider in making home visits on your own congregational members. (They work best in the order given.)

1. **Pray** before you get out of the car.

2. **Introduce yourself** at the door and ask if you can have 15 minutes of their time. Respect their wishes if they say "not now," but that will rarely happen.

3. **Establish rapport** by finding things you have in common, such as art, attendance at the same special events, struggles with the weather, living space, pets, etc.

4. **Deepen the relationship** by inquiring about his or her faith story, spiritual history, relationship to the church and the Christ (or lack of one!). Ask such questions as: "How is it being a Christian at St. Luke's?" or "How has your relationship to the Christ changed over the years?"

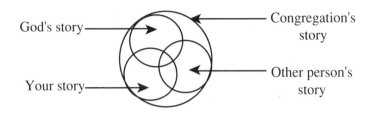

5. **Provide an opportunity to ventilate feelings.** A question like, "What suggestions do you have for our ministry together at St. Luke's?" can provide a good opening for people to express their feelings. Be sure to take notes to take back to the church for follow-up.

A usable step at this point might be to inquire if they have an unchurched family member or friend or work acquaintance whom they would invite to church or permit you to invite. (Remember every one of your church members have between five to seven people like this they know and these are by far your best prospective members.)

6. **Give a brief spiritual message** about the season of the church year, e.g., the hope and anticipation of Advent; the surprises of Epiphany; the forgiveness of Lent; the starting over of Easter; or the Spirit's presence of Pentecost.

7. **Extend an invitation.** Offer a specific, one sentence invitation to take a next step in their discipleship; e.g., "I would like to invite you to serve on St. Luke's Stewardship Committee," or "Would you join me in organizing a new witness task force next Sunday at 3 p.m.?"

If the answer is no, rephrase the question so it can be answered with a yes, like, "Will you pray for me as I work to get a stewardship committee going?"

8. **Pray out loud** for those in the home and those absent, but in the family, using their names. Hold before God a summary of the visit, listing the things discussed.

9. **Leave** mentioning when you will next look for them at worship, church school or whatever.

Summary

The above thoughts I had while flying from Chicago to Oakland were simply perceptions and a methodology that worked well for me over my years in the parish. I was in some large parishes where the senior pastor was not especially expected to make hospital calls, but it was deeply appreciated when he/she did. I felt it essential to my preaching and ministry that I do so each week, no matter how busy I might be with other administrative and ministry tasks.

Having the reputation "if he/she knows about it he/she will be there" is a very good thing for any pastoral ministry. People like to know they can count on your being there and bringing the comfort and compassion of Christ to them so they will not have to face a crisis alone.

I am sure that no other pastor would agree with every one of the above suggestions! Our personalities are different and we would go about our ministries, to which God has called us, in different ways, equipped with God's spirit. However, let me say again, do go, be a presence, take the sacraments and pray.

Pastor As Preacher:

Proclaiming The Good News

The Preacher's Edge

The older I get, the more convinced I am that God created preaching as much for the benefit of the preacher as for what happens to the congregation. Could it be that in the divine scheme of things we have been equipping, instructing and encouraging *ourselves* even more than those who sit at our feet when we preach? Could it be that this is what God intended all along? We go into our pulpits with zeal and a sense of mission to proclaim the gospel to our congregation, when all along through God's spirit, God is inspiring *the preacher* with a sense of mission.

Several years ago when I was on sabbatical in Liberia, West Africa, there was a worship service at the Bong Mine parish conducted by missionaries Barry and Alice Lang from Canada. The public-address system was rather antique, but the electricity was on at the moment. When it came time for Alice to lead a song about the power of God, she picked up the hand-held microphone so that she might be heard. On that damp, rainy morning, the microphone, which was not grounded, shorted against her moist lips. Barry told me that her hair stood on end, her eyes bugged out, and she shook all over. Those several hundred Liberians gathered there for worship were heard to say, "Dammy, Mamma Lang! Dammy, dammy, dammy!"

I believe there is that kind of power available to us in our pulpits, also. I call it the preacher's edge.

Could it be that God had:

> The preacher of Ecclesiastes preach so he could gather the wisdom of religion, thus better equipping himself to teach the people?

> Noah preach righteousness in order to convince himself he was right about God when he seemed so alone?

Peter preach at Pentecost to give himself a boost after the Ascension when Jesus was no longer physically with him?

Paul preach so he might reinforce his own conversion to the Christian faith and overcome his own doubts?

Barnabas preach in order to equip himself to do much needed peacemaking?

John the Baptist preach so that he might be convinced to repent, as well?

Jesus the Christ preach in order to reassure himself that the kingdom was still very near?

Martin Luther, John Calvin, John Wesley preach so that they might remain strong in their call for reform at a time when they seemed so alone?

We have the privilege of power from the pulpit like all these saints of the church who experienced the preacher's edge. The power is as close to us as it was to Alice Lang. Our hair doesn't stand on end, our eyes don't bug out and we don't shake all over. And so, the change and charge that are possible never really happen to us or those to whom we preach.

Before The Sermon

Just think what it means to us preachers that we preach week after week, Sunday after Sunday, in our congregations. Think what it means that we have to prepare for that sermon ahead of time. We have the luxury of searching the scriptures and studying its implications for ourselves as well as for our people. It certainly means we have the discipline of weekly distilling our faith into words understandable to us and our congregations and restating the glorious good gospel over and over again. It also means, at a regular time each week, we can give careful thought to our congregation's needs and refocus our ministry and our own lives, as well.

In preparation we certainly discover guidance for our lives as we prepare to give advice to others. We learn how to deal with selfishness, greed, temptations, ego mania and the other real life, close-to-the-ground struggles. As we prepare to advise others, we gain insight on how we should behave, as well. We have the luxury every week of quiet time, solitude and rest from the hassle of daily ministry. It's almost like a spiritual retreat when we get to feed on the scripture and dialogue directly and anew with the Almighty. As we prepare to preach, we are refreshed, refocused, and reminded of life's priorities. That ought to improve our parenting, our marriage and our coping with loneliness, as well.

And think how we are kept in tune with the life and presence of Christ as we follow the church year in our sermon preparation:

the expectation and hope of Advent;
the wonder of Christmas;
the surprises of Epiphany;
the forgiveness of Lent;
the new life of Easter; and
the inspiration and spirituality of Pentecost.

As we go into that period of time called sermon preparation, we learn once more who we are and what our relationship to God, who called us to preach, can be. The others in our community view us as holy people who speak directly for and with God.

We also have the chance to reflect on our practice of ministry as we prepare to address all the lay ministers of the congregation and see that they are well-equipped to do the ministry they are called to do through their baptism. All this is in the preparation to preach. We haven't even gotten to the pulpit yet!

During The Sermon

But let's consider what happens to the preacher as he or she actually delivers the sermon. I recall that high, up-in-the-air

81

pulpit at St. Paul's Lutheran Church in Greenville, Ohio, where I grew up. My parents would stay after church every Sunday and hang onto me as they talked to what seemed to me like everybody in the congregation before we could go home. Once in a while I would break loose from their grip and run for that area in the church forbidden to children: the chancel. And on the rare occasion when I would get through the chancel before my dad grabbed me, I'd make it into that massive pulpit! My dad would then have to corner me, grab my arm and jerk me out of the pulpit, explaining that only Reverend Wessel went there. And, indeed, he did go into the pulpit and was a changed person every time. When he preached, no one sat in the first four rows in front of that pulpit because he sprayed saliva all over them! He was a man of enthusiasm, energy and excitement, and it seemed as if walking into that pulpit electrified him so that he could bring the gospel to the people with intensity and fervor.

One of the major things that happens to us when we preach is what I call empathy transference. To me, it means love making between preacher and congregation. Those people so want us to do well, and they love us and tell us that through their eyes and body language. This becomes a very intimate time with God and God's people where we are embraced and caressed by God's spirit and by God's people as we communicate back and forth, pulpit to pew and pew to pulpit. In that empathy transference, a bonding also takes place. It's good to know that we are loved and cared for and that's communicated to us as we preach. We feel revered and loved just as we are, with all our imperfections and trepidations.

As I was growing up, my mother always developed a nervous stomach whenever I would do public speaking. I think she still does when she is in the audience. I had similar feelings when my sons played football or my daughter performed on the harp. And when our youngest, Sarah, was the first girl to play boys' Little League in Richland County, Ohio, our entire family would sit on the bench to make sure that our "second base person" was treated well. And so, when we preach, our congregational family empathizes with us, as well.

We get a rush of inspiration and a sense of being in the special presence of the Almighty — and in these days of drugs and alcohol, that's a legitimate high!

One of the real surprises about preaching is that we will probably be better at it than humanly possible. I am sure of this! We can actually be much better than our human skills, education and experience would allow. That's the work of the holy spirit which surrounds us, lifts us up and is the preacher's edge. In other words, we are lifted out of our human limitations to experience the thrill of God taking over and speaking through us.

There is a second place and time when we have a bonus to our preaching that is simply unexplainable in terms of human communication. Not only is there that edge that causes the preacher to be better than he or she is capable, but there is also the edge in the hearer's interpretation of what is being said which is far better than what was preached! How else could one explain those comments at the door about the sermon which the preacher didn't realize he or she said ... and may not have. For God's spirit enables each hearer to interpret the preached word through that individual's life experience, further boosting the significance of what the preacher had intended to say and giving him or her an edge.

Preaching is also a time of affirmation and respect that gets us through the week. Like those who cheer in the stands cheer for a football player, and help get him through the second half, so too the congregation cheers for their pastor, helping him or her to get through the week.

There is enough fear about standing in front of this group that it gets the adrenaline moving and the heart pumping, giving our bodies the energy and strength we may have not thought we had. Any public speaker, singer, musician or actor will tell you about that "edge" and the importance of getting it as they begin to perform. A bonus is that we can be creative and experiment and risk and fail without fear of trying again the next week.

Yet another luxury of the pulpit in preaching is the catharsis of exploring frustrations. It's a good mental health process for us to be able to release our anger and to experience the thrill of being frank and bold about ourselves. There is a form of group therapy that goes on when we preach to a congregation who knows us and whom we know.

The verbalization of our fear can also occur. In counseling it's called ventilation. Any preacher in touch with his or her congregation will work through and bring to the surface repressed material of his or her own. Whether that be done consciously or not, it's mighty healthy. Of course there is a danger of that taking over the sermon, but the fact that it is risky is also part of the value of doing it. Hence, preaching can benefit our own mental health. It can lift us out of depression as we work through problems and pump an exhilarating and fresh feeling into our own being, as well as the congregations'.

After The Sermon

Not unlike applause feeds the ego of a performer and gives encouragement to risk again, so the comments, greetings and handshakes at the door give us immediate positive feedback. It's almost instant gratification. We gain larger doses of affirmation and expressions of love and caring than we really deserve. But it does help and that gives us strength to go out and do our best for these people of God again.

And we really have said things beyond our human capacity which now can be printed. Editors also advise those of us who publish our sermons never to compose the final draft until after preaching it. They evidently have learned that there is something extra which happens in the actual preaching of the sermon. They want us to capture God's contribution as our own profundity for the final product.

Our preaching adds to our own certainty of the gospel. Like someone who whistles in the dark and begins to own the behavior of being brave, so we preach with intensity and become even more convinced of the good news we proclaim. And the more convinced we are, the better we convey the message. Our character has now changed because of what we have preached so we become it and believe it. I remember a classmate at Wittenberg University who was a good actor and played the part of King Lear in a Shakespeare drama. He was a Stanislaus "method actor" and he so became the character of King Lear that he never broke out of it the rest of his life! While that's a drawback to method acting, an advantage is that we can so preach in a way in the pulpit that it can become a part of who we are from then on.

Implications For Preaching

If you accept my premise so far of what happens to us when we preach, I'd like to continue by listing seven implications of preaching:

1. The process, including preparation and delivery, ought to be filled with prayer. We must learn how to open ourselves to God's spirit; that is, actually drench ourselves in God's presence until we are filled with the spiritual. That fullness spills over and inundates sermon notes and sermon proclamation.

2. Expecting great things to happen allows for that edge of God's surprises in our preaching. After all, the real serendipity of preaching is the joy of it!

3. It will help to be free from manuscripts in order to allow for God's contributions to the sermon content and for the eye contact with God's people to love and encourage us so that they can draw us out as the spirit wishes.

4. We will want to always compose our sermon notes and practice our proclamation preaching to ourselves, as well as to the congregation. And we must never publish our sermon in printed form until after preaching it so that the inspirational edge to the content can be made.

5. We ought always practice out loud in the holy place where we preach to encourage the spirit to begin and continue the possible inspiration.

6. We will practice a certain reverence for the pulpit as a holy place where miracles happen in us when we allow them and the congregation encourages them.

7. We need not see the preparation to preach and preaching as grim duties, but as marvelous opportunities and "edges" in our ministry which deeply benefit us, as well as our congregation.

No wonder God calls us to preach:

> our people sit with us like my family did when Sarah was "second base person;"

> we have great opportunity to work through our frustrations and ventilate our feelings;

> there is an empathy transference between us and the congregation;

> it's a wonderful luxury of retreat each week to prepare in God's presence; and

> we have an edge which makes us far better than we really are.

So, like Luther, Jesus, John the Baptist, Paul, Peter and Noah, we preach and we are changed because of it. Perhaps that's what God intended all along.

"Dammy, Mama Lang! Dammy, dammy, dammy!"

The Sermon On The Amount

One of the more frightening tasks we preachers have, particularly as we're getting started in our parish ministry, is preaching regularly on the subject of financial stewardship. For some reason a myth prevails that there is something sacred about our money and we shouldn't mention it from the pulpit. As a matter of fact, if we put a fence around the pulpit and do not address financial stewardship, we are eliminating about two thirds of our congregants' lives, lifestyles, worries and that subject about which they are most interested in hearing.

Here are some ideas I have about preaching that "sermon on the amount." It ought to be done well and with confidence as a witness from us and the Almighty to our people.

We ought to talk about our own struggles and need for growth. That way we are not preaching down to our congregational members, but rather are inviting them to join us in thinking through this subject and trying to grow with us.

Let the message be Bible-centered. I always made sure that I read the scripture in the pulpit from a Bible I could hold in my hand so that visually people knew where the message was coming from and what was my source of authority for saying what I was saying. Be very careful about proof texting. Especially in stewardship preaching, it is easy to prove what you already wanted to say by looking up Bible verses that support it. Rather, take one of the great parables, miracles or sayings of Jesus or Paul, or other early saints of the church, and let your message flow from that.

I doubt that we get very far by emphasizing duty when it comes to stewardship! I think it is much more effective to talk about the joy and privilege that is ours who have so much and for whom God has done so much and given so much, to be able to give to others.

Be sure to use specific terms which everybody understands, such as cash, dollars, credit cards, checkbooks, IRAs, savings accounts and so forth. I think that "time, talent and treasure" is an old chestnut that's out of date!

Be very careful not to scold, lecture or belittle. Speak very kindly and non-judgmentally. Try to accept everyone where they are and then plead in a very persuasive way for some growth.

Be sure to use sizeable doses of humor and refrain from heaping on more guilt. It's so easy to harangue and build guilt on our people because they are not doing what they should or not doing what you are doing. Humor is good relief from that, and it is also a very persuasive and consistent method of teaching about the gospel with its privileges and responsibilities.

This means using the law very sparingly and talking a great deal about gospel with great delight. Let enthusiasm show through. We ought to allow the spirit to set us free to preach with conviction and excitement about this wonderful subject that can give such significance and integrity to our lives.

By all means, if we are like most preachers and rather uncomfortable talking about the subject of stewardship in the pulpit, we ought to tell our people that. Pastor Don Hillerich reminds us that this serves to relax our listeners and they will take more seriously and less defensively what we are trying to say. They'll love to hear us admit that we are human and that this is rather frightening for us to do, and they'll root for us to do it well!

Encourage reasonable increases in growth and Christian giving. Don't use examples that people will feel are unreachable. Acknowledge where **you** are and what **you** are trying to aim for, and plead for them to get started in growing too. Pastor Hock recommends that we ". . . stress increasing gifts by one percent of income each year, with tithing as a goal." He notes that this works.

Much of the above would not be frightening, and certainly our preaching would have more integrity and relation to the gospel, if we dealt with the subject of stewardship year round.

This means to talk about the subjects of stewardship of all God's creation as caretakers of the earth and its resources, of our own bodies and health, of our abilities and skills, and of our call through our baptism to be ministers all week long. The possible subjects can go on and on, and it can enrich our preaching, making it much more relevant than ignoring the matter except for one Sunday during the year.

Be very careful about making appeals of loyalty to church, preacher or budget. This kind of stewardship pledging and giving is often very fickle and short-term. It is much more important that we talk about each person's *need to give* rather than an institution's *need to have* what we give. In a culture like ours, we do have a big need to give lots of our income away in order to experience the integrity of being a Christian and to feel good about our priorities. Just be sure that God's love shines through and that the wonderful amazing grace that we talk about in every other facet of our lives is also applied in our stewardship and stewarding.

Be cautious about promising results such as prosperity or making an appeal to give because "we never had it so good." It could be that some seated there and others who will hear your message are not having it that good right now!

One of the main responsibilities in financial stewardship preaching is to lift the vision and stretch the possibilities, and help the congregation imagine what might be as we all work together to grow in this concept. Remember that people give in proportion to their grasp of the need, the quality of information provided, the amount of spiritual depth and motivation they have, the financial resources they have to share, and/or perhaps from your own example.

We often forget in our preaching of any kind of sermon to suggest to our people the possible first steps as a result of that which we have learned in this instructive sermon. I call it the "so what!" of a sermon. Think through carefully what it would mean for each of us, because of these truths that you proclaim this day, and let your people hear it.

Several times a year in our preaching we have to remove the mystery regarding the writing of wills and doing estate planning and setting up trusts and endowments. We need to convince our people that this is, indeed, an easy thing to accomplish and a good practice of stewardship of our resources in order that future generations continue to benefit because of our depth of faith and our willingness to share.

There are few things that can so enrich preaching and make it relevant and exciting to do as practicing the art of stewardship preaching year round. In a culture such as ours where money talks and is the language of all the media and our lives, in order to be close to the ground in our preaching and also faithful to the scripture we proclaim, we must continue to preach the sermon on the amount.

The Children's Sermon

For whom do we give the children's sermon? What is the message we are attempting to convey? And, most importantly, why do we do it at all?

After preaching 1,400 children's sermons, I am not sure that the message we give can be learned by the ones who come forward for it. I doubt they will even remember it for the remainder of that day, and I am certain the purpose must be more than the content of the message. Still, congregations demand that children's sermons be given and often comment that it is the most meaningful and understandable part of all the verbal messages in our worship!

After observing many students and pastors trying to satisfy their congregation's demand for children's sermons, I am convinced that some ought never give them. In fact, as a homiletician, I am not even sure that a student can learn to do children's sermons very well. Some seem to be born to the task. Truly, it is more like a gift than a set of acquired skills. The weariness I experience with a lot of the children's sermons I hear leads me to advise that some preachers should take advantage of someone in the congregation (like an experienced pre-school teacher) who can do it well, and then sit with the kids and listen.

Neither am I sure that those young people who come forward for the sermon have the capacity to relate the utilized object to the lesson or truth the object is supposed to illustrate. However, I do believe the object ought to be used as something to focus on and to playfully wonder and talk about.

After all these years of giving children's sermons, I am convinced that the time is probably best spent in helping children feel included, valued, important and loved in and by the congregation. Hence, it is more important to provide a certain "feel of it" than to get content understood. It is a time for the pastor to bond with the children of the congregation. It is the children's time in the liturgy when the congregation acknowledges they are a part of God's family, and it is a time when God's love and that of the people around them — especially their pastor — is communicated to them.

Pastor Wong advises that "it is possible to improve our children's sermon skills by consulting a good pre-school or elementary school teacher and learning about children's development." He adds, "Do not set high expectations for mental understanding, the key is experience."

The time might even better be named, "Children's Time," when the children look forward to some fun and playfulness within the setting of the worship experience and when they have friendship demonstrated and expressed to them. It will be a time the children anticipate each week that is for and about them.

Of course, overhearing does take place. It is an opportunity for the adults to hear further illustrative material about what will be proclaimed in the other sermon of the day. Certainly the children's sermon ought to support that one and recognize the theme of the liturgy and worship.

The children's sermon is not a time to display how cute children are. With this in mind, we need to pay particular attention to which way the children face and which way the pastor faces. We must also note the pastor's posture to be sure he or she does not tower over the children, yet still conveys the office of pastor. Some pastors kneel to speak and others sit to be at their level. My advice is to not ask questions or force an enthusiastic "good morning" if they do not want to do that.

Story is probably the best form for a children's sermon. The old-fashioned flannel graph or the opportunity for children to act out the story in the Old Testament or Gospel for the day is still a very effective way of communicating and enjoying a certain playfulness and creativity during the children's time. Bishop Robert Miller adds, ". . . and don't moralize on the story after telling it."

There are other ways we might consider helping children to not just endure, but actually enjoy, coming to church.

Booster chairs such as those used in restaurants, stacked up at the door and available for the children as they go into the worship area, can enable them to see more than the back of a pew and observe the activity in front of the church, and thus enjoy the service more. The old-fashioned "children of the church" when young people are dismissed during part of the service for their own special worship opportunity still works. Many parents enjoy worship without having to tend to children the entire time (or part of the time). Most growing congregations find that a Sunday school held at the same time as worship works very well.

Why we do it, to whom our message is addressed, and what that message is are all crucial questions to be considered and answered as we decide whether or not to call young people forward for a children's sermon.

Pastor As Administrator:

Organizing For Mission

Working With
Church Governing Boards

It is very complicated and yet extremely important as a parish pastor to work in mission with our church governing boards. Keeping them focused on their minstry in tandem with yours is not easy. Keeping a vision for the congregation's mission and ministry in front of all the people is crucial.

In the musical, *Fiddler on the Roof*, Tevye sings, "If I were a rich man ..." I'd like to rephrase the words a little and say, "If I were on a governing board..." I'd want to be sure:

1. There had been a very thoughtful and prayerful process in electing me. I would want to be certain that when I was installed it was in front of the congregation and a dignified public announcement of the ministry which I was about to share and the governance role in which God had called me to serve.

2. I had opportunity to study. I would expect that the pastor would provide me with at least one book a year to read on congregations and ministry, that I would have weekly Bible study guidance, that I would have a working knowledge of the denomination's social statements, and that the doctrines and confessions of my church were well explained and I was given opportunity to learn them.

3. I knew the larger expression of the church. I would want to know much more than just the local congregation and community. I would expect my pastor to teach me about the churchwide expression of my denomination, as well as its global mission and ministries.

4. I got instruction in witnessing to my faith out loud all week long and my pastor took seriously seeing that I had continuing opportunity to grow spiritually.

5. I had specific, measurable and attainable goals which I could set in cooperation with the rest of the council and my pastor.

6. I got help in developing a meaningful prayer life individually and corporately.

7. I was expected to disagree at times with other board members and board leadership in debating important issues and respected for it.

8. I had a good system for fellow members to communicate their suggestions to me. I would also expect there to be a small committee of the congregation headed by a board person which would be called "pastoral relations committee" or "mutual ministry committee" or something similar, which would meet regularly with the pastor and provide counsel and input to him or her.

9. I had a partnership with the pastors in actually doing ministry, as well as supervising ministry. It's a fine line, but we need to continually work at empowering our lay people to do their own ministry in daily life all week long, as well as meeting monthly to supervise the congregation and pastor in his/her ministry. A congregation like this would mean that the pastor would empower board people to call on the elderly, make evangelism calls, do private baptisms, do disciplining of new members and carry out advocacy in the community.

10. My time at meetings would not be wasted! I would want to be sure that an agenda was always provided with those items on the agenda that had the potential of taking lots of time being marked, and that the meeting was conducted in such a manner as to keep focus on the topic at hand.

If I were a board person, I **wouldn't** expect to:

1. Micro-manage the parish.

2. Have my input ignored when given individually to the pastor or in the church governing board meeting.

3. Have expectations put on me I am not equipped to do, thus causing me to fail or lose face.

4. Have to sacrifice my family life for my ministry as council person.

5. Give up my integrity in order to have consensus in the group.

6. Be expected to do many things poorly, rather than one or two things very well.

7. Do the work of committees or task forces in board meetings, rather than their bringing crisp and precise recommendations to the council after careful consideration in the committee.

Every governing board person ought to have a written job description when they are asked to serve so they can look it over before giving their answer if they will serve and so that they have something by which to judge their performance as they do serve.

It's very helpful to have a yearly retreat for the council when, along with the pastor, goals can be set and planning can be done for the coming year and the longer vision of mission for the congregation can be brought into focus.

Include spouses in at least one social event of the board people a year to give them ownership in that to which their spouse gives so much time.

Do lots of coaching of your governing board committee chairs. In larger congregations, it works well to get the committee chairs together before their meetings and have all the committees meet at the same time. This pre-meeting of chairs can gain advice from each other and have a sense of purpose and clarification when they conduct their committee meetings.

A planning session with the chair of the board or the officers of the board before council meetings and after the committees have met works very well. This gives the leadership of the board a good idea what issues will be coming before its meetings and helps them strategize how to conduct a helpful meeting and structuring an agenda for it.

Have all governing board members on a mailing list of institutions that are supported by the congregational budget through its individual support or its benevolence to the nationwide expression. The denominational magazine, newsletters put out on particular subjects, such as parish programs, evangelism and stewardship ought to be included. The seminary which is supported by the congregation should have a list of all the crucial people so they too might provide timely information about that which is so important to the life of the congregation in the future. A judicatory newsletter should come to governing board persons as well.

Try to find ways to protect a governing board person's worship experience from complainers. It can be a miserable experience for those serving on the governing board to come to worship and have people continually approach them with complaints when they are trying to have a good worship experience.

It's always a good idea to have minutes taken carefully and approved by the board at their next meeting and often can be well received by placing them publicly on a bulletin board so the people of God can see what transpired at the last meeting. Sometimes it works better to do a summary of what occurred at the meeting and print that in the newsletter, rather than putting out the specific minutes that might contain confidential information.

One of the things we often fail to do is thank the governing board persons when they are finished with their term of office. There does need to be closure so that a person can feel good about his/her contribution to the life and governance of the congregation. A special meal when a certificate, plaque or small token of appreciation is given and public thanks expressed will help the governing board person celebrate his/her time of service and remain a faithful, positive contributor in the congregation.

Other important issues and trends that church governing boards will want to explore for their congregations in the 90s are as follows:

1. **The ministry of the laity.** We believe that all Christians are called through their baptism to do ministry in the world where they work, live and play. One of the main tasks of a church governing board and pastor is to empower the laity to carry out that ministry in the best possible way. This means to practice gift identification. We must help all of our lay people learn what their natural gifts and skills and abilities are and what particular chrisms the spirit of God has provided them. The next step is to identify where their kind of ministry is most needed in their lifestyle and routine. This will probably

be one of the main emphases of ministry in most mainline denominations in the '90s and beyond. Rather than be threatened by the ministry of the laity in daily life, clergy ought to be thrilled that they can be the instruments through which God empowers this person to do ministry in this powerful way.

2. **Discipling** is a response to the great command Christ gave the disciples on the Mount of Ascension before bodily departing. We have an obligation and privilege to empower our people to follow Christ as a disciple. This is far different than the world's priorities and means a heavy emphasis and understanding of stewardship of all creation and evangelizing of all God's people. A congregational governing board that places a heavy emphasis on discipling will make sure that at least once a year witnessing instruction takes place for all the people, Bible studies are offered in enough different formats that all members and friends of members might have opportunity to study, the class that prepares people for membership goes far beyond building loyalty to the institution of the church and moves them to loyalty to Jesus Christ and his commands, there would be one-on-one coaching of each other in discipling and there would be provided very specific spiritual direction for all those willing to receive it.

3. **Motivating the passive congregation.** The book by Lyle Schaller titled *Activating the Passive Church* is very helpful in moving the majority of our congregations from inactivity to activity. Perhaps a congregation is now out of the mission mode and comfortable. Because there have been many unmet goals or the congregation is now focusing on celebrating anniversaries and its past rather than envisioning and planning for its future, the congregation becomes passive. We can move our congregations out of this state by accomplishing and celebrating small victories, listening to the angry and disapointed, thanking the folks who have tirelessly given of their time for years with little appreciation, and emphasizing the strengths that are already there in the parish. It does mean that we develop a participatory process of developing a mission statement and doing a long range strategic plan that propels the congregation into the future.

4. **Moving from survival mentality to mission mentality.**
Many of our mainline congregations have regressed into a state
of survival rather than mission. In a new book by Daniel Buttry titled *Bringing Your Church Back to Life*, Judson Press,
Valley Forge, 1988, we learn that people view congregations
in very different ways. Buttry lists the following as basic defi-
nitions of congregations by their individual membership:

A. **A Club.** People gather to be with other like-
minded people and have a good time. The members gather
mainly for their own sake and benefit.

B. **A Massage Parlor.** The church is a place to come
and receive comfort, to be made to feel good.

C. **Alamo.** An outpost surrounded by a threatening
and hostile world. The physiological wagons are pulled
into a circle, and the defenses go up.

D. **A Theater** that specializes in old classics. The
church lives in an era that is long gone. It becomes out
of touch with the present. It is no longer powerful and
pertinent, but is merely interesting to those who like that
era.

E. **A Museum.** A place to preserve memories. Most
of the remaining members are curators of the memories.
In a survivalist mode, living too close to the realities of
the decline with its shrinking membership and shriveling
finances.

F. **A Nursing Home.** The church becomes a haven
for a few elderly folks until they pass on and the church
finally dies with them.

5. In the '90s we'll need to think in terms of new paradigms
in almost all instances of setting program. Win Arn, of Monrovia, California, in his *Growth Report* newsletter, lists many
new paradigms for various traditional programs of ministry.
Here are those that he suggests in the following categories:

OLD PARADIGMS	NEW PARADIGMS

Evangelism

Confrontational	Relational
Mass	Personal
Single method	Multiple methods
Goal: A decision	Goal: A disciple
Church membership	Christian discipleship
Motive: Guilt	Motive: Value and love

Pastor And Staff

Enabler	Initiator
Activity-oriented	Vision-oriented
Selection based on	Selection based on
credentials	performance

Christian Education

Sunday school	Small groups
Age graded	Lifestyle graded
Verbally oriented	Visually oriented

Facilities

Considered adequate	Regularly upgraded

Worship

Presentation	Participation
Intellectual	Experiential
Focus on Christians	Focus also on non-Christians

Volunteers

Sacrifice self	Maximize self
Members serve institution	Institution serves members

Denominational System

Resists change	Insists on change
Centralized	Regionalized
Bureaucracy	Accountability
Served by churches	Serves churches

6. **Attention to the extended congregation.** The days are past when we may expect people to show up at the church and all we have to worry about is whether we are welcoming them properly and showing a warm, good experience once they get inside! This is especially significant when we realize that in the U.S., in most communities, each one of our present church members knows from five to seven unchurched people. Since these folk are by far the best prospects for witnessing and bringing into the church, we can begin to program and budget our evangelism efforts in productive ways.

The great majority of people who join churches in the '90s will be people who have some connection to someone who is already in the congregation and who has invited them to visit. This means especially that new members need to be equipped to witness to their faith and to invite those they know who are unchurched and live in the congregation's service area.

While it takes considerable skill to work with church governing boards, it can also be one of the delights and joys of any pastoral leadership. Without forming an unapproachable clique, we can develop a close, Koinonia fellowship of our governing boards and a shared ministry with them, so that the full potential of God's spirit might be experienced in our mutual mission and ministry.

Ministry With And To Committees

Using congregational committees wisely in order to carry out the mission of the church calls for much intentionality and skill. While it is not always true that the best way to get ministry done is by using a committee, the following may be helpful to you in working with them.

In General

Be sure to include new members of the congregation in the committee membership. This brings in new ideas and some fresh questions that may not have been asked for a long time. The same is true of including youth on each committee of the church.

It's important that the church governing board change the chair of the committee each year (or every two years, at most). This change in leadership often lends new stimulus to the committee's sense of mission, and also demonstrates a collegiality that can be valuable in church work in general.

When recruiting members for any committee, and especially for the chair of the committee, it's important that they know the limits of their terms. This means that they know when they are finished serving on the committee and exactly what they are to accomplish so they can identify it when it is done. A written job description will help. A well-functioning committee will set goals early on and work toward those goals during their time together as a committee.

Be up front about the budget and the amount of money the committee has to use in its endeavors. This ought to be understood right away as it makes for much better stewardship of the church's resources. It also keeps a committee from making ambitious plans only to have them scuttled by the finance committee or treasurer. That demoralizes and embarrasses a committee into inaction.

In general, it is very important that each committee sees what its part is in accomplishing the mission of the congregation. This means having a congregational mission statement that each committee can use to direct its goal and evaluate the focus and effectiveness of its ministry. Often the goals for the committee can be set as objectives assigned by the church governing board to that committee to fulfill as a part of the overall mission statement of the congregation. If a committee knows what it is authorized to do and to whom it is accountable and has good, thorough education, it can provide a satisfying ministry for its members and perform a good ministry in the parish.

In medium to larger-sized congregations it is often very effective to hold all committee meetings at the same time. This allows the pastor or lay leadership to conduct worship for all committee members assembled, after which each committee can meet separately. It also frees up other nights for the pastor's other ministries. As pastor, you can circulate among the committee meetings to answer questions or to simply be available for any inquiries.

One of the advantages of having all the committees meet on the same night is that committee members get to see each other and recognize the size of the task and work force for the mission of the congregation. Another benefit is that members of various committees can consult with each other at the time of the meeting, and thus make more enlightened decisions.

Ahead Of Time

Having someone on the committee call each member to remind them of the meeting will always make for better attendance.

Providing an agenda worked out in consultation with the chair of the committee will lend focus to the meeting and will also help to accomplish a great deal more in the limited amount of time. Meet with the chair before the meeting begins to work

106

out goals and objectives and set an agenda so you're ready to go when the committee members arrive. Note: It is not wise to meet just for the sake of a meeting. Be sure there is a valued purpose for meeting and a sense of accomplishment when finished.

Be sure to set the beginning time and the ending time of the meeting and stick to it! This single principle will help improve attendance over the long run, perhaps more than any other one thing you can do.

Give some attention to the amenities before people arrive for the meeting. Arrange the chairs so everyone can see each other as they meet. Providing a refreshment evidences preparedness, hospitality and respect for the work of the committee members.

At The Meeting

Always begin with brief devotions and prayer.

At the first meeting, be sure to take time to get acquainted. This will pay off in big dividends during the rest of the year.

Ask a member of the committee to keep notes of each meeting. This need not be as formal as taking minutes in most cases, but serves to remind people of decisions, discussions and future aspirations of the group.

For most small committees and congregations, it works best to **not** follow Robert's Rules of Order when voting yes or no on issues. With a little patience, a committee can usually arrive at consensus and everyone feels better about the decision.

Don't talk about poor attendance at the meeting. Simply celebrate those who made it and accomplish as much as possible with their advice and help. Assure members that their time was well spent, helpful and point out the progress they have made.

After The Meeting

A telephone call to those who did not attend the meeting will usually be appreciated if it is done tactfully and shows real concern for their absence. Mailing a copy of the meeting notes to absent members will be deeply appreciated. It also shows that you take their membership seriously and want to keep them up to date on the activities of the group. Post the meeting notes on a bulletin board or summarize them in a church newsletter. Try to avoid the appearance of a clandestine or secretive committee meeting!

Anna-Marie Klein adds to this chapter: "There can be a terrible pull to get the pastor to do everything, be everywhere, fix everything. Borrow from the business world in learning to delegate, stick to one's true task, keep a schedule so you are available at known times.

"Learn about volunteerism from the books of Marlene Wilson, a national expert on volunteerism in the non-profit setting. Attend or set up a volunteerism workshop in your area.

"Build on the congregation's strengths. Involve members in committees (and short term task forces) where they serve with comfort and are at their best. Catholic churches near me have 70-80% of their congregations involved in one way or another (may be a prayer group, not a committee) and are thriving in spite of the great lack of clergy."

Stewardship Of The Facilities

While we readily think of the word stewardship as applying to the amount of money contributed by our members through the offering plates, pledge cards and monthly checks mailed in, we rarely think of it in terms of maintaining our facilities.

When you are a pastor of a congregation which uses a building for its worship and out of which its mission is organized and carried out, you need to think in terms of being good tenants, stewards or caretakers of that facility, not only so future generations will have full use of it, but in order that the facility be well maintained and used in the most efficient and effective way possible in the present.

A large building and other facilities can be a tremendous drain on a congregation's budget and mission. It is easily possible to so concentrate on the building that we forget our real purpose of doing mission in the kingdom. On the other hand, deferred maintenance and poor caretaking of the facilities can mean that future generations of pastors, church councils and property committees will have to pay dearly for our neglect.

The following are some of the categories you can consider as you think through what it means to be a steward of the facilities of your congregation. By listing these categories and projects, I don't mean to indicate that you need to do them all! But you do need to realize that in order for the congregation's laity to take on any of these projects some encouragement, leadership, knowledge and direction from you will be necessary.

Stewardship of Energy and Water. It pays to have an energy consultant do an inventory of all electrical appliances and recommend what ought to be installed in their place. New electrical appliances such as ballasts for fluorescent lighting make it possible to cut energy consumption by between 20% and 28%. Incandescent lighting is almost always the most energy-consuming lighting to use. High-pressure sodium lighting outside will not only provide more candle power, but can also save considerably on the electric bill. Electric companies in some states have a rebate system whereby nearly the entire cost of replacing the incandescent lighting with new and less energy-consuming fixtures can be paid for from the rebates.

Converting starters on furnaces from gas pilot light to electric will also save energy consumption. Have a company check out your furnace to determine the level of operation efficiency. Old furnaces run at about 60% capacity; new, as much as 90%!

Timers installed on heating and lighting equipment can be large energy savers. Because so many people fail to turn out lights and lower heat, timers can do the job. It also pays to do zoning of heating and cooling so that the entire building doesn't need to be heated or cooled when small groups meet in a room or two. Additional economies and conservation measures can be had, too.

1. In colder climates a lot of attention ought to be placed on sealing around doors and windows, especially those that fit loosely and can easily be corrected by using weather seal strips.

2. In church sanctuaries or assembly halls with high ceilings, the installation of a few ceiling fans which will force the hot air back down to the floor will save those heating BTUs.

3. Have a couple of insulation companies check out how well you are insulated and how you would be rated for the need of additional insulation.

4. Hot water heaters ought to be wrapped with a special blanket (obtainable from hardware stores) to save energy.

5. Watch out for leaky toilets and faucets. A lot of water can be wasted by failing to replace washers and tighten plumbing joints. One brick placed in the toilet tank of each toilet will save water consumption with each flush, which saves a lot of water over the long haul.

6. For landscaping in hotter climates, converting from a water system which sprays on top of the ground to an underground drip system will save considerable water.

General Maintenance. Have your property committee tour the facilities several times a year and make out a list of projects to be accomplished by volunteers and professionals. Plumbers, electricians, general contractors, housekeeping and landscape people make excellent members of such a committee.

It pays to have a professional company do an inventory of the entire facility and its contents. This will come in very handy if you need to justify a settlement with an insurance company for fire or water damage. Minimally, every congregation ought to have one of its members who has a video camera take pictures of the inside of each room and its contents, as well as of the outside of the building, including the stained glass. This will be a tremendous help in case of fire, tornado, wind or earthquake damage. Of course the information should be stored off-site or in an on-site fireproof file.

There are professional companies that will diagnose the roofs of your buildings and give you recommendations for any required maintenance. Be sure that all rain gutters and drains coming from the roofs are open and working so that the water does not back up and it drains away from the foundations of your building, avoiding severe damage, such as building settling.

Almost every stained glass window company is willing to do an inventory of your windows and give you a bid on what needs to be done to maintain them well. In urban settings, it often pays to place Lexan storm windows on the outside of the stained glass to protect them from destruction (and in colder climates to provide a dead air barrier between the two windows, which serves as good insulation).

Organ service companies can be contracted with to inspect the church organ on a regular basis and make recommendations for its service. It pays to keep the organ well maintained, as it gets very expensive to repair if you let it go over a period of time. Blower motors and billows need lubrication on a semi-annual basis.

All wood exposed to the elements ought to be sealed and kept painted, especially in those areas of the country where there is considerable moisture.

111

Blacktop, which is used for parking lots and sidewalks, should be treated with a sealer once a year to prolong its life. Jenite is usually used. Don't allow it to be sprayed on, but rather use volunteers to apply it on a hot day with large squeegees.

Your insurance company will provide the names of companies which will inspect your boiler annually. This is important for safety and efficiency.

With your volunteer or paid maintenance person, work out a year-long chart to schedule lubrication of all pumps and blowers and to change or wash filters.

Do not disturb any asbestos which might be on furnace pipe wrappings, in asbestos tile on floors, or in some insulation. Usually you can get by with just seeing that it is not disturbed, but in some cases it ought to be encapsulated so that the asbestos fibers won't circulate in the building air system.

It pays to have a contract with Johnson Control, Honeywell, or a similar company to service the heating and air conditioning controls regularly. This will save wasteful consumption of heat and cooling.

Damage to buildings from nearby trees can be kept to a minimum if they are kept trimmed. In some cases, they may need to be removed if fire, wind, or ice storms, or root intrusion would cause them to damage the building.

Keep tubes of caulking on hand to reseal the glaze around windows. In buildings located in colder climates, any crack or opening where water can get in and then freeze ought to be sealed.

Look over your building on the outside and see if tuck pointing (the regrouting around bricks or stones), sealing of exterior cracks and silicon waterproofing ought not be done.

If engaging a sand blasting or hydro blasting company to clean the exterior of the building, make sure it's a reputable one! If sand blasting or hydro blasting is done in warmer climates, walls ought to be mildew-proofed. In colder climates or where there is considerable moisture, water-proofing is important to reseal the newly-cleaned walls.

Safety and Security. If you are in an area where earthquakes are possible, it is very important to anchor buildings to their foundations and make sure that shear walls are in place. All hot water heaters ought to be strapped to the wall and flexible piping used to plumb the gas source. Failure to do so is one of the major causes of fire in an earthquake.

For safety, use iridescent tape and mark all steps with stripes. People with vision problems will find this especially helpful. Use a non-skid wax on all floors where people might slip, especially in entrance areas where people sometimes enter with wet shoes.

Snow and ice should be removed around the church buildings and on all walkways. This is important not only for convenience and safety, but also to send a signal that this church (congregation) is thriving and open for business, is user-friendly, and attends to its environment.

Electric heat cords installed in the rain gutters on a church building will help prevent ice from building up and falling on people and sidewalks. Be careful about any location where downspouts empty out on the sidewalks. This water can create a hazard if it freezes.

Be sure that plenty of lights are installed outside your building, both for better night vision and prevention of robberies. This is also good public relations and raises the visibility of your church in the neighborhood.

Tree roots can damage sidewalks, causing unevenness and hence a tripping hazard. Remove roots as necessary and repour concrete sidewalks if damage has been done. Plant trees well away from walkways and buildings. In urban settings the city is usually responsible for this work if the trees are between the street and the sidewalk in an area called "the parking."

All glass doors ought to be marked with tape so people don't try to walk through them. This is a very common and often serious accident that takes place in institutional buildings.

Much of the maintenance of our facilities can be done by volunteers. There are those in the congregation who, while unable to contribute much monetarily or in areas of public speaking, teaching or witnessing, are very willing and eager to contribute and take part in a "work day" or give time each month to work on facilities maintenance. In congregations that observe a church year, an "all paints day" can be fun and will get a lot of painting done.

Your congregation will benefit by keeping a property log in which to record any work done on the church property. In this way you always have a history on the facilities for future congregational leaders to use. When walls are open because of remodeling, or ditches dug up, etc., take a picture of the work location so future generations will know how it was done.

In the urban setting where crime and vandalism are a threat, I have found it advisable to convert one or two Sunday school rooms into a small apartment and house a person there to take care of security and oversee maintenance. This can reduce the number of break-ins and helps the congregation feel more secure, especially when they come to the church for an evening event.

Fire Danger. Poor electric service seems to be one of the main causes of church fires. Replace old fuse boxes with breaker boxes so that ample service is provided to all the facilities and circuits are not overloaded.

Install a functional fire alarm system in the building. In urban settings it is often possible to combine a security system with a fire alarm system and have it hooked up to the local fire station.

Fire extinguishers should be provided throughout the building, well-marked and maintained. Your local fire department is usually willing to inspect your buildings and make recommendations for improving fire safety. Be careful where you store gasoline and other flammable materials so as not to add to the risk of fire.

If outdoor fires are a threat, it is important to remove any shrubbery or decking that might serve as a "fire wick." Dry shubbery on which a fire can travel or in which sparks can set a new fire and spread to the building is especially dangerous. Keep roofs free of pine needles or dry leaves. Don't permit trash dumpsters to be stored next to building walls.

Have a set of fireproof files in your building for your church archives and important documents. Of course, copy the very important and valuable items you will want to store in a safety deposit box in another location (e.g., a bank), but a fireproof archives may be a great blessing, as well.

When you are able to move from a mode of crisis maintenance ("fix it when it breaks") to preventive maintenance, you become better stewards of the beautiful facilities former generations have provided for the congregation. This frees up more money for ministry, gives a better impression about the importance of the mission, and promotes a better attitude toward the institution when we, as stewards, care well for the facilities.

There are many resources in a community that can help in seeing that you are a good caretaker of the facility which has been given to you to use for a while for God's mission. Now that you are in a leadership position, you must be a good steward so that future generations can benefit and continue the mission which you presently enjoy.

Pastor As Program Resource:

Maintaining Mission Emphasis

Theology And Witness

We have opportunities in the '90s to do outreach in a special and effective way and need to reexamine our reasons and motivation for doing evangelism.

Why should we be concerned about evangelism and outreach? Evangelism is commanded by Jesus in those verses of Matthew 28 called the Great Commission. Notice there that we are not only to baptize but also to teach and make disciples. I think we have often taken the baptizing much more seriously than the teaching and making disciples, and yet discipling is one of the ways in which we bring people to the need for their baptism. Making disciples certainly seems very consistent with God's mission for us in our world. Foundational in our ordination is the mandate to teach. We pastors must be faithful to this call to discipleship and discipling.

Because in our culture in the United States we can no longer depend on ethnic groupings or emigrants of a particular nation and their children to make up congregations, we have a need to fill the ranks of the workers and worshipers in our congregations. That is reason enough to reach out to all the unchurched!

Pastor Nachtigal demurs from this statement: "The fact that we need workers and worshipers to help us seems , to me, **not** to be reason enough to reach out to the unchurched. If there is an implication that we will dwindle without them, then it seems that our enlisting of the unchurched is just selfishness. You [the author] have said this many times, and it has come to my ears as comfort and grace: 'Let *mission* shape the institution.' Telling the love of God in Christ and letting that love change people's lives is a different mindset than gathering in the unchurched to keep our church going."

Evangelism is a matter of the health of the congregation as well. The more we share the faith the more real it becomes to us and the better we are able to share it. That wonderful

119

circle of sharing and being strengthened to share can help the stability and health of any congregation.

To enable our membership and our clergy to witness to their faith helps our spiritual lives as well. As we see new members come into the Body of Christ by allowing the Spirit to work through us, it deepens our sense of self-worth and we have a sense of fulfillment and accomplishment.

Don't forget that the unchurched have a desperate need for the forgiveness, love, mercy and guidance which God can give them through the Church. Our culture is one of wealth addiction, self-centeredness, greed and tendencies toward unhealthy families and neurotic lives. To become a part of Christ's Body (the Church) can turn us away from self-centeredness and provide an alternate lifestyle that is much more fulfilling and pleasant to practice in these days.

Remember that our theology is full of God's grace and the fact that it is God who saves us, not our own cleverness. When we contrast this with other sisters and brothers who try to frighten people into the Kingdom by threat of hell and eternal torture, we see yet another reason to bring our kind of theology as a gift to people who have been turned off by the faith of others.

In Martin Luther's catechism in the meaning of the second article of the creed he says, "... I believe that I cannot by my own reason or strength come to Jesus Christ or believe in him ..." God has worked it out that the Holy Spirit will work through us. We are the instruments through which God decided God's grace would be shared.

There are some points of entry right now in the '90s that we must consider as opportunities and take advantage of them as we try to remain faithful disciples and follow the Christ.

1. **Discipling new and current members** of the congregation is our greatest opportunity to do outreach. New members received into the congregation are our best evangelists. They have large numbers of acquaintances who are unchurched and live within our congregation's service area who can be invited to join. We must take our new people beyond loyalty

to the congregational organization to faithfulness to the call of Jesus Christ to be a disciple. That means they must be taught how to witness to their faith out loud to others and be good stewards of all God's creation. Not only does this give us an opportunity to equip those newer members to be evangelists and stewards, but also gives us an opportunity to move them beyond a rather shallow organizational loyalty.

2. **Offering witness instruction** at every possible chance in the congregation is another opportunity for outreach. This means confirmation classes, women's groups, church choirs, church councils, youth groups, young adult groups, organized Sunday school classes and many others. We already have many organized groups and if we deliberately make sure they know how to witness to their faith we already have a large force of people ready to do outreach.

3. **Finding ways to activate our passive congregation** is still another entry point for doing evangelism. Some have estimated up to 80 to 90% of the congregations in the U.S. are plateaued in their membership growth, declining, or in a state of passivity. This means we need to find the ways to avoid that decline in membership and passivity and move it into a growing congregation again. This kind of growth is described in the book of Acts in the early Apostolic church. Good strategic planning, teaching of witnessing, sharing the leadership power with new members, celebrating some small victories, and turning toward a visioning posture rather than one of fortress or survival mentality can make a big difference in a passive congregation. Understanding where our congregation is in its life cycle will help us analyze what is taking place and what we can do about it.

4. **Evangelizing the web of the congregation** is yet another important entry point. Church growth advocates like Win Arn have taught us about doing outreach: each member of the congregation has from five to seven people who are unchurched that they know who live in the service area of the congregation. These people are best targets for outreach. Those who know them are by far the most effective people to invite them.

This extended congregation ought to be on our mailing list, and we ought to spend one out of ten dollars of our budget on programming and ministering to them. Each one of them who is received into the church brings another whole web of acquaintances who are our best prospects for new members.

5. **Discover the present strengths of the congregation** which is where we always want to start. A new pastor is often asked to do those tough things that the other clergy could not do or simply neglected. Instead, we should concentrate on that which we can do well. We also want to ask new members why they joined the church and, if we see there a trend of something that's working for us, then use that strength to lead out with everything we can.

6. **We ought to practice better conservation of the mobile Christian.** While we do make some effort in bringing people into the congregation who have moved into the service area, we rarely spend very much energy on seeing that the member who moves out of our service area into the service area of another church gets settled into that congregation. It's a matter of membership conservation and a matter of good churchmanship that we do this.

The New Testament gives us many examples of witness, especially by those who saw Jesus face to face: Andrew went after Peter; Jesus sent out the 70; James and John could not refrain from preaching what they saw and heard; and Paul traveled country-to-country witnessing to the Gospel.

We, too, have God's equipping spirit which empowers us to be disciples, to make disciples, and to witness. Jesus promised those first disciples: "... you will be filled with power when the Holy Spirit comes on you, and you will be witnesses for me in Jerusalem, in all of Judea and Samaria, and to the ends of the earth." — Acts 1:8.

For a longer treatment of specific suggestions on doing outreach in our parishes, consider my 1993 book by CSS, *Called To Witness*.

Christian Education

A Theological Perspective

We, who are disciples and follow the Christ, have certain responsibilities. Because God is the creator of all things, we practice stewardship of the whole creation. Because God redeemed us in the person of Jesus the Christ, we practice evangelism and share that redemption with other people. Because God continues to save and sanctify, we practice Christian education so that we might continue our growth in grace and maturity in the faith.

Sanctification is the spiritual process of moving beyond being saved for eternity to learning more of God's will for our lives. This is a word not often used by Christians, but it certainly does call for a lifelong intentional process of allowing the spirit to work in us so that we might mature and grow in our knowledge and discipleship of the Almighty. Martin Luther wrote in the meaning to the third article of the Apostles' Creed in his catechism: "... but the Holy Spirit has called me through the Gospel, enlightened me with his gifts, and sanctified and kept me in true faith. In the same way he calls, gathers, enlightens, and sanctifies the whole Christian church on earth ..."

Parish pastors and Christian educators have the responsibility and privilege to be the instruments through which that Holy Spirit calls people to the Gospel and enlightens them with the Spirit's gifts. We are also instruments through which that spirit continues to sanctify (make holy) and keep us in the true faith. Church school classes, vacation church school programs, weekday school, Bible studies, retreats and other educational enterprises of the congregation enable the spirit to "... call, gather, enlighten and sanctify."

Jesus told his disciples to: "... go and make disciples of all nations, baptizing them in the name of the Father, the

123

Son and the Holy Spirit ..." — Matthew 28:19. Our Lord sets the example as teacher and rabbi. He also asked us to make disciples, and that calls for a very intentional educational ministry!

In our rite of the Affirmation of Baptism (confirmation) we Lutherans lay hands on the heads of the confirmands and pray for their "growth in grace." While that very rite which many denominations practice is the culmination of an educational process called confirmation, the rest of the Christian's life is to be a pursuit of continuing to mature in the faith and the wisdom of God.

Through our baptism we are called to be ministers in the world. That means we need to be equipped and to equip others for a ministry in daily life. It takes education and reflection in order that we might grow in our faith and be faithful ministers in response to our call. Luther informed us that we were to be "little Christs" to our neighbor, and that, too, takes education. Those who are ordained have a call to "*word* and sacrament.*" Education is one of the primary ways we open up the word of God to others who have been called to minister to and love on God's behalf. The main line Christian denominations have a special responsibility to provide an alternative to some of our sisters and brothers in other denominations that suggest that you "check your brains at the door" when you enter the church. We can provide the educational process and the opportunity to do discipleship which is compatible with an intelligent understanding of the universe.

Some Observations

Discipling may be the most important educational ministry that we have. This means intentionally moving the Christian beyond institutional loyalty to a faithfulness to their call by the Christ to be a disciple in the world. The pastor should be a prophet, priest, pastor and teacher. This means the pastor should always teach. Often the clergy person is the best prepared theologian in the parish and not to share his or her knowledge with others in the congregation can be a waste.

In projecting the future by looking at present trends, I would guess that public schools will continue to cut budgets and churches may very well be the center of the humanities, arts and music. This will open up many new educational possibilities in our parishes. Because of the negative influence of our more conservative and fundamentalist sisters and brothers in the public school systems, Christian education may have to provide much needed human sexuality education, as well.

Certainly, vacation church school is still the best community outreach opportunity! No pastor should divorce him or herself from it. Plan to be there, visit it and teach at every opportunity. By creatively promoting the VCS, we can always bring in some of the unchurched in our community and service area. (The service area being that area within a reasonable driving distance from the church building.)

I think Christian day schools can provide a great opportunity for minstry and outreach. Some would claim that in order to be the "salt of the earth" and "the leaven to the lump," we need to be in the public schools. That certainly needs to be heard and considered. But it could be that we can provide an education for our young people in the Christian setting which is more inclusive, global and unafraid to deal with religion, integrating it throughout the curriculum.

The present baby boomers want their children to have the Christian education they had, but they will want it to be very convenient! They'll probably demand that church school be held at the same time as church, if they are going to worship at all. These generalizations may no longer be as true as they once were.

Because of our pluralistic society and wide varieties of lifestyles, we will probably need to look at having two Sunday school sessions each Sunday morning, a pre-school or day care service all week long, a weekday school (which may be best held where people are during the week, rather than at the church facility), and some kind of school of religion, which will allow the retired and younger adults to seriously study the Christian faith.

About having two Sunday school sessions, Pastor Nachtigal writes: "For most parishes I highly question the feasibility of this. Not impossible, but, with renewed interest and understanding the need for education in the parish, the first point to be made is that Sunday morning is a two-hour experience: worship and education. Is it unrealistic to think that if both worship and education are top-notch and if the lay people are in the middle of planning and follow-through, that people will be there? And if the pastor is leading with vision and energy. Perhaps relevance is the question more than convenience."

Depending on the size of the congregation, some possible Christian education opportunities that a parish might consider offering are first communion classes, Sunday church school, confirmation ministry, short-term and long-term Bible studies, weekday school of religion, vacation church school, Christian kindergarten or pre-school, retreats and other tailor-made multigenerational educational events when the culture and congregation calls for them. If it is a smaller congregation, it sometimes can be a joint venture with other nearby congregations.

Some Mistakes

I believe it's a mistake to count on the public school teachers in our parish to do the teaching in the educational programs. I found that the public school teacher is tired of teaching by the end of the week, and to pressure him or her in church school is counter-productive to good teaching and learning. They can, however, serve as a resource, sharing their professional skills on teaching, classroom arrangements, creative methods, understanding different age groups and handling discipline problems.

It's also a mistake to give signals that Christian education is just not all that important to people. Those on the education committee and those who teach and administrate will communicate how significant it is in that parish. The size of the budget, the condition of the facilities, the schedule of events, and especially the pastor's involvement will further communicate if this has a top priority in the congregation.

In my opinion, many church school facilities are overbuilt and underused. This is poor stewardship. In many congregations, the poor condition of rooms and equipment sends the signal that Christian education just isn't very important.

I don't think it's a good idea to shut down church school during the summer. It is a time to be even more creative in how the church school operates. Shutting down church school in the summer, while continuing to have worship year round, suggests that we "take a vacation" from education!

Be careful about automatically accepting anyone who volunteers in the Christian education program. Rather, focus on recruiting the very best teachers available. Do avoid depending on the women alone to do the teaching. Use couples or teams to do teaching whenever possible. Take advantage of intergenerational education; summer Sunday school and vacation church school are wonderful opportunities to bring all ages together and experience education together.

The lack of appreciation shown to teachers and church school workers is shameful! We frequently make the assumption that they will serve forever! Allow for terms of service. At least once a year in the worship service, take time to celebrate Christian education and those who give so much to it. We ought to set the theme that teaching is a calling.

Pastor Hillerich shares what works for his parish: "We use the quarter system. Our teachers teach for 13 weeks at a time. It is very exciting for our parish. Teachers are willing to give us the 13 weeks. We have installations four times a year."

Failing to provide and require ongoing teacher training is another trap that is easy to fall into in any congregation, especially in those where there is already a full program. We must keep in mind that wrong ideas can be taught in our church schools by very nice, well-intentioned people.

Don't fall into the trap of using a hodgepodge of curriculum material. Often a denomination will have a lifelong learning grid worked out for when certain basic things will be learned. To insert another curriculum may cheat the student out of ever covering certain theological and Biblical truths that are important to developing discipleship and the process of sanctification. Of course, you will want to critically evaluate the curriculum and adapt it to your specific context or setting.

Many clergy make the mistake of modeling their teaching after what they saw in their seminary. Sometimes seminary professors have no education in pedagogical procedures at all. Usually we can do better than what we have seen in the seminary classroom! Pastors need to learn to be teachers.

It is also a mistake to leave out the spiritual dimension from the educational experience. How the offering is received, how prayer is used, and reverence for scripture will be noticed, remembered, and internalized.

Whatever you do, don't underestimate the social value of Bible studies and organized classes for adults. The "communion of saints" is real in our congregations and often that little turf which has been staked out and furnished by a small group of people called an adult Bible class is very precious to those people. Be careful about upsetting that "communion of saints."

There are a number of ways in the parish that we can completely divorce church school from church worship. That is a mistake. We must try our best to integrate worship and the educational experience when reporting to the congregational council, setting up committees, scheduling worship and education, and during many other occasions. Often a sermon series preached by the pastor on the church school themes being studied by the students will provide the right kind of reinforcement and integration of learnings.

Many congregations make the mistake of being unwilling to spend the kind of money that will provide good teaching equipment and facilities. That kind of economy rarely is productive in a parish and can send a signal to the congregation that Christian education just isn't very important.

Perhaps the one large mistake that many of us clergy and educational professionals make is to fail to see the "teaching moment" in all activities of the parish. Worship and liturgy, preaching, architecture, music, social ministry, new member education, stewardship, evangelism, first communion, baptisms and rites of the church, all offer opportunities to teach.

Often, in an event that is reported in the papers and which is on everyone's mind, makes an excellent opportunity to talk about its theological implications. Most students only learn after they see the need to know what is being taught. When those moments occur, we need to sense them and experience the serendipity of jumping in and teaching.

Creation, redemption, sanctification. We are stewards of that creation, witnesses and evangelists of that redemption, and teachers, through which sanctification — the spirit of God — works. Let's continue to be the instruments through which God's spirit "... calls, gathers, enlightens and sanctifies."

Sexuality Education

We who call ourselves religious have tended to pervert God's wondrous gift of sexuality, perhaps even more than those who are promiscuous. Certain over-enthusiastic Christians have distorted God's priceless gift by teaching a form of reasoning that sounds biblical, but is quite contrary to the whole context of the Judeo-Christian scriptures. They reason that what is spiritual is good and what is of the flesh is evil. From that they extrapolate the idea that because sex is of the flesh, it is therefore evil.

What more fitting place is there for our young people to be taught about and nurtured in a healthy sexuality than in the church or synagogue? In an environment where people care about each other and each other's wholeness, one can come to best understand his or her sexuality. If the young don't learn about it from us, they learn it in the locker room or from graffiti and pornography. Every young person is getting an education about sex and sexuality someplace or another — and of one quality or another.

The Christian community believes that God created us in God's likeness — male and female — and that God saw ''that it was very good.'' So, essentially, sex is holy and healthy as our creator intended. If it be evil, it is only because we misunderstand or abuse this natural God-given drive.

I believe God is concerned about the whole person, which includes body and soul, physical and spiritual. We are created sexual beings and are largely conditioned by our maleness and femaleness as long as we live. Those zealous Christians who consider sex to be inherently evil berate God! I just can't imagine a good and loving God creating us with natural desires that are dirty, evil and uncontrollable. So, it is only when we come to see our sexuality as a priceless, God-given gift, that we respect it, and keep it for its God-intended purposes.

Fundamentals Of Human Sexuality

1. Sexuality is of God, therefore it is good and beautiful.
2. Sexuality is a driving motivation of our personhood.
3. Sexuality is that which attracts us to others. It is among these persons that we may find that one person to whom we would want to commit ourselves for love and for life in the covenant relationship of marriage.
4. We must assume personal responsibility for the gift of a sex drive because we are accountable to God for it, just as we are with any other gift.
5. Sexual feelings are natural and necessary. They are not evil, but these natural feelings are to be kept within the purposes of God's intentions.
6. Sexuality is the means God has provided wherein we may express our deepest spiritual feelings (love) in a very tangible way to our partner in marriage.
7. Sexuality warms up all that may grow cold in marriage. It keeps two people re-attracted to each other.
8. Sexuality provides tenacity and romance, both of which are essential to marriage.
9. By means of our sexuality, God has provided the opportunity for us to be co-creators of human life.
10. Sexuality can be the realization of our identity and fulfillment.

The religious community, given to teaching the truth, needs to teach our children the truth concerning sexuality. Truth never has to be feared. Some people think if children are taught about sexuality, even though it be the truth, it will make them promiscuous. Yet, it is the *lack* of knowing the truth and facts about sex that *contributes* to promiscuity.

I think there is a particular relationship between our spirituality and our sexuality. Those with the healthiest spirituality seem to enjoy the healthiest sexuality. Those with an unhealthy sexuality cannot seem to acquire or enjoy a healthy spirituality.

Similarly, sexuality and personality are very much interrelated. If one's attitude toward a sexual relationship comes

131

from regarding this expression as a treasured gift from God, meant to nurture marriage and the family, that attitude will permeate that sexuality.

The Judeo-Christian community teaches that love and sex go together. As soon as you separate the two by a double standard, you fracture the human person, who is a unity of body and soul.

The Bible insists that love doesn't seek its own end but seeks the fulfillment of the loved one. Those who exploit their sex drive primarily to satisfy themselves may never grow beyond childish, genitally-focused relationships.

It is important for us to realize that sexuality in marriage is not exclusively, or even primarily, for parenthood, but for partnership. Two people in love marry so that they may be, first and foremost, husband and wife (real marriage does not need children to hold it together). The Judeo-Christian community recognizes that sexuality is what matures the partnership. In turn, parenthood is usually no better than the partnership. Sex is sacred. It is to be revered and enjoyed, just as God intended.

Our Task Is Large

I don't think we parents are doing the job we claim to do when it comes to sexuality education. We have a God-given mission to help our children think through their sexuality. We need to apply the time-tested principles accepted in other areas of education to sexuality education: to equip youngsters with the skills, knowledge and attitudes that will enable them to make intelligent and moral decisions for themselves.

I think it's through our church institutions and our families that we should carefully, sensitively and thoughtfully, relate to our young. We need to nurture them in a healthy sexuality, getting them to recognize that sex is more about *above* the belt than below! It originates primarily in the head and heart rather than in the genitals.

Sexuality education programs, then, must begin with adults. It must begin with parents-to-be together. If a child's basic sexual attitudes are largely formed in the first years of life, waiting until school age to teach them is much too late. One of the church's biggest tasks is to open communication between youth and parents. In my own parishes I found that the most productive time during sexuality education was when I helped the children formulate questions to ask their parents, which in turn would provide an opportunity for them to talk about the subject openly. When church and parents work together, sexuality education is most effective.

Pastor Denton-Borhaug makes this observation about teenagers' need to discuss their sexuality: "I have found that, given the chance, the teenagers in my congregation want and need to talk about sexuality. The boys want to talk with young male leaders of the church; the girls want to talk to me. Listening, acceptance, valuing people and encouraging them to value themselves and see themselves as beloved of God — all of this is important. I have been utterly horrified by the quantity of sexual abuse I have come across in my relatively tiny congregation, and see this as a crucial issue the church needs to address. I have often found preaching to be a valuable method of letting the congregation know that I am willing and open to hearing about these painful issues of people's lives."

Issues Related To Conception Control

The decision for or against having a child will include evaluation of such factors as:
•The physical and/or emotional health of the potential parents
•A reliable prognosis concerning the health of a possible child
•The number and spacing of other children
•The family's economic circumstances
•The rapid growth of population
•The family history of genetically-related diseases
•A history of untreated abuse: physical, sexual, emotional
•A history of drug/alcohol addiction

People have a right not to have children without being accused of selfishness or betrayal of "the divine plan." *Every child has a right to be a wanted child.* Everyone is entitled to receive information about conception control from governmental and voluntary agencies. We, as loving Christians, also have a responsibility to provide and see that public education provides solid educational tools regarding sexuality and intimacy, family counseling and education, welfare services and birth control/family planning services.

In my parish programs, I found it especially helpful to provide sexuality education beginning with the kindergarten age through high school every year in the church school program. I simply made announcements ahead of time that we were going to do that in each class for a period of five weeks in a row, usually in early summer, and the parents responded by making sure that their children were there. These were some of the best attended church school classes all year long! People even brought their neighbor's children to such classes.

We used medical personnel, usually the congregation's doctors and nurses, teamed up with clergy and laity who felt comfortable in doing the teaching. I met with the teachers ahead of time and conducted a day-long workshop on the subject. We provided them material that offered, with few exceptions, an excellent curriculum for the entire age span.

In addition to the above, my wife and I held an annual retreat at the end of August before school began for our parish's fifth grade youth, spending an entire day talking with them about human sexuality. This is a good age for us to convey an honest and open attitude, letting those children know what we knew about them and that now they knew about us. Perhaps the greatest contribution of the day was establishing an open channel of communication between pastor and youth. There were many times later when those same people would talk to me about very personal ethical sexual problems because they knew that I was approachable and knowledgeable.

The main goal of working with these fifth graders was to get some basic information across, debunk some myths that they believed about their sexuality, establish an open relationship with me as pastor, and open up communication between them and their parents.

Pre-marital sexual education also needs to take place. Even though many of the young people we now marry and most of the older folks who are being remarried have already been living together, I believe it essential to require some pre-marriage sexuality counseling. Often, there are so many wrong beliefs and, on God's behalf, we can enrich the marriage relationship by giving good information and helping both male and female get in touch with their most basic feelings.

Listed here are some admirable goals and guidelines that a pastor can establish, and ones that have informed my ministry. Some of these might be considered controversial, but please consider them carefully:

1. Hold a retreat for the parish youth on human sexuality at about the fifth or sixth grade level. (Planned Parenthood contends that youth acquire their "sex education" by this age from other street sources, if not from parents or the church.)

2. Continue classes and discussion through high school on the subject.

3. Require pre-marriage counseling for all for whom you perform the marriage service.

4. In struggling with the issue of abortion, particularly during the first trimester of pregnancy, I hold that there is a difference between a fertilized egg, a fetus with a developing brain, and a full-term baby out of the womb with the possibility of relationship to other humans and Christian baptism.

5. When doing personal counseling, explain and encourage the use of birth control. I encourage no intercourse outside the bonds of marriage, but explain that if that cannot be accomplished, the use of contraception is highly recommended.

6. Ease guilt about masturbation. This is a very common phenomenon and ought to be explained to our children so that they do not grow up with submerged feelings of guilt about that which most do anyway.

Some Tips On Parenting

Always use the correct words. Sharpen your vocabulary and try to diffuse dirty words. Use accurate words to describe body parts and functions so that as the child matures, he or she gets a healthy and natural picture of it all.

Work on having the kind of relationship with your children where you are approachable for questions. Let them know that we share something very special by our sexual functions and our knowledge about them. Talk openly about sex and reproduction, when appropriate.

Provide good materials to read and use. Use whatever opportunity you have to teach about sexuality, such as television programs, pets having intercourse and reproducing, new babies arriving, overheard conversations explained, and the daily newspaper stories.

Anna-Marie Klein writes: "Use natural times when parents seek group assistance and learning — the beginning and end of confirmation time, for example. Use these opportunities to the fullest because parents often are abandoning their children at confirmation time — emotionally and spiritually. Church guidance is generally accepted by parents at these crossroads — and is a vital time for the Christian life of parent and child."

Relate God to human sexuality and reproduction. Try to emphasize that sex is good and a gift from God when experienced in marriage.

Don't give the idea that sex or body parts are evil or dirty but are to be enjoyed. Be careful about how menstruation is explained so that a healthy attitude of the miraculous is conveyed to those who hear it. The subject of masturbation should be handled in a similarly positive fashion.

Get over your own embarrassment. Debunk all the myths and acknowledge the strong sexual feelings of teens, helping them develop good humor about it. Share the struggles and feelings you experienced at their age. (Be careful here, because it is a rare young person who wants to hear the old saw,

"This is the way it was when I was your age . . . !") Stress that Christians exercise the covenant of fidelity and view the female with honor and respect, as opposed to an object to be conquered. She, like the male, is to be regarded as a full person.

Be absolutely certain in the day of AIDS and of promiscuity promoted by the media that you equip your young people for responsible sexual behavior. Tell them how we are different from the rest of the culture that's reflected in the media.

Things I Don't Believe

1. I don't believe that all sexual intercourse is for the purpose of procreation. There is a difference between procreative and relational sex, and we ought to celebrate and recognize the differences.

2. I don't believe that original sin is passed on through sexual intercourse (a heretical doctrine called Tradutionism).

3. I don't think that having a marriage license constitutes a Christian marriage. There needs to be a life-long covenant of fidelity to make those bonds significant and God-given. Most denominations have a service for blessing a civil marriage.

4. I don't believe enjoying our sexuality is dirty, evil or wrong. Maleness or femaleness should be enjoyed. We ought to recognize and find good humor in our God-given and natural urges.

5. I don't believe that sexual gratification can take place only with the opposite sex and only through vaginal intercourse. Certainly, masturbation is a reasonable solution to being alone, if that is necessary.

6. I don't believe that we should legislate the type of sexual behavior that two consenting adults practice in the privacy of their home.

7. I don't believe that the marriage state is any more "right" in God's sight than singleness. Certainly scripture never tells us to get married! There is a fulfillment of God's purpose for us in being single as well as in being married.

8. I don't believe that remarriage is any less blessed by God than a first marriage.

9. I don't believe that sexual intercourse between two unmarried adults is different than when one or both are married. Marriage is a life-long pledge of fidelity to each other. When either goes outside the bonds of marriage, it is a serious sin against God's plan for us and for our marriage promises.

10. I don't believe that homosexuality should be condemned as an unpardonable sin. Biblically, it is viewed as a departure from the heterosexual structure of God's creation. But, homosexuals are sinners only as are all other persons if they are alienated from God and neighbor. It is essential to see such people as entitled to understanding and justice in church and community.

Things I Believe

I think it is within the permanent covenant of a marital fidelity that the full potential of coitus is realized to foster genuine intimacy, personal growth and the responsible conception of children.

Sexual exploitation in any situation, either personally or commercially, inside or outside a legally contracted marriage, is sinful because it is destructive to God's gift and a human's integrity.

We presently live in a male-dominated society. I don't believe God is pleased with the present distortion of males subjecting the female as a lesser person. Treating females as less than males is a sin and distortion of God's creation. This should especially not be true within the hierarchy and clergy of the Christian church.

Let the above thoughts be a call for us who claim to be God's people, and who often teach a sort of distorted, unbiblical sexuality, to repent and begin anew to rediscover the marvelous gift we have as the sexual beings God created us to be and enjoy.

Note: While the entire manuscript on "Sexuality Education In The Parish" reflects my own strong personal convictions, I am not yet certain that each of the thoughts included is entirely my own. I am including this chapter in my *Plane Thoughts On Parish Ministry,* but continue to research the possibility that not all the material is original. I dictated this chapter from notes in my notebook that I used to make a major presentation to Planned Parenthood of Iowa several years ago. I am usually very meticulous about writing down any material I have copied from other sources. There are none in my notes, and I am hopeful that I have not used someone else's material and failed to give that person credit. I believe the material to be my own, but am not absolutely certain yet and will continue to search.

JLS

Social Advocacy

In addition to our role as priest and pastor, we have also been called to be prophets in the world. As Jesus showed a special preference for the poor, outcasts and social misfits of his day, we must take the part of those who are less fortunate than us and for whom racial injustice, prejudice of all kinds, and often unjust circumstances have enabled others to oppress them.

Formal Advocacy In The Parish

We already have many opportunities in our congregations to advocate for the less fortunate. We can conduct adult forums on social issues during the church school hour each week. We can take our young people on tours and involve them in work camps in the midst of the oppressed, and we can organize visits to our state capitol and talk with the legislators and their assistants who make the laws that protect or oppress the disenfranchised of the community.

If we are within driving distance of the state capitol, special speakers on the legislative agenda can be invited to visit the congregation and present the issues faced during that particular session.

Holding one- or two-week work camps in inner city parishes or third world countries offers a tremendous experience for both the youth and adults of the parish. Mini retreats away from the church building on social issues of justice can be profitable, as can bringing in special speakers to church school classes.

Of course, our prophetic role ought to be evident in the pulpit if we do it in a way that doesn't divide the congregation and reinforce already deep-felt prejudices. There is a way of proclaiming the good news that encourages people to examine themselves on touchy issues without forcing them to leave the congregation if they disagree with the preacher.

Having a congregational task force on advocacy, separate from the social ministry committee, is very valuable. Often, social ministry committees find themselves so occupied with the organizations and agencies of the church and their causes, that they have little time to look at the bigger picture and talk about issues of justice.

Of course, we want to follow the calendar of the national expression of the church and observe social ministry month, using available printed material.

It's also a healthy thing to bring social issues and our recommendations concerning them to our church assemblies. The congregational members will get informed in producing the motions and will serve a prophetic role as a congregation.

Belonging to a political party was very helpful to me. It put me on the inside where I was more likely to be heard and taken seriously.

Informal Advocacy Opportunities

We can only be effective as prophets in our parishes if it is obvious that we love and care about our people. Befriending legislators and talking with them frequently can influence their input into the legislative process. Being a friend of the city council people, attending council sessions frequently, and living within the city limits so we can address the council, all are important ways of making our voice heard.

In my own ministry, I found a role in serving as private counselor to those in power, particularly in the state legislature and the public school system. Befriending these folks and lending an open ear is a way that eventually leads to being able to confront them with theological questions concerning the issues they must decide. These power people who make the important decisions in our culture are often befriended in the local service club.

Try having a worship guest one Sunday a month when you bring in someone in a leadership role and simply introduce him or her as your guest. This gives your guest a chance to become aware of you and the congregation, and also helps the congregation see what that guest's ministry is all about.

Serving on boards and in agencies such as Planned Parenthood, National Association for the Advancement of Colored People, and a group I started in Bellefontaine, Ohio, called Committee for Racial Understanding, was an effective way to influence a community to see that those who did not have their voices heard were protected. Belonging to such causes as Amnesty International, the Sierra Club or the League of Women Voters not only communicates our beliefs and values, but also our intention to be part of the solution.

One of the best ways we can make sure the Christian counsel is heard in our culture is to convince good lay people from our congregation to run for office and then support them. That is indeed a ministry of the laity that can make a difference!

As I look back over my years of parish ministry, I think of some of the opportunities that I experienced as a parish pastor. Serving as the chair of the board of directors of the Lutheran Inner Mission Society of Springfield, Ohio, let me be on the cutting edge of race relations and integration of communities and my own congregation. Serving on the Mayor's Committee (and getting others in the congregation to do so) for such concerns as drug abuse and pornography proved valuable. Aligning myself with the fundamentalist group that ran a nearby shelter for homeless men gave me an opportunity to witness to my ecumenical faith and also to head a drive to build a new shelter when the old one was abolished from downtown by the politically powerful.

I was able to make the biggest impact by getting appointed to the Ohio State Reformatory's Citizen Advisory Committee while I was a pastor in Mansfield. That led to being on the governor's Penal Reform task force for the Council of Churches of Ohio. Serving on the board of directors of Wittenberg University and Grand View College allowed me to speak with some clout about divestiture of their endowments in multinational corporations operating in South Africa businesses.

Being pastor to one of the leading scientists at Drake University in Des Moines allowed me to join him in battling the creationists who were out to change the wording in all the science textbooks in Iowa to support creationism.

When Ohio's Seneca County board of supervisors started a regional planning commission, I was able to serve as its chair, helping to organize it and take hold of environmental, planning and transportation issues in that area.

Pastor Robert Hock writes about the above list: "Don't imply we should do all of these things! Just some!" He's right.

The list of possibilities to serve goes on and on. The pastor has to be very careful about over-committing him or herself in community causes and organizations. But once getting connected with the organizations, you can see to it that your lay people gain positions of power where a consistent and effective witness to social issues, their causes and possible right solutions can take place. I now wish I had spent a little less time myself doing social advocacy and more time empowering my lay people to do it.

When Jesus first returned to his home synagogue, he was asked to preach. The scroll of the prophet Isaiah was handed to him and he read these words: "The spirit of the Lord is on me because he has appointed me to preach good news to the poor, he has sent me to proclaim freedom for the prisoners and recovery of sight for the blind, to release the oppressed, to proclaim the year of the Lord's favor." — Luke 4:18-19

He asks us to do no less. When our ministry is finished, let it be said of us, as he said to them, "Today this scripture is fulfilled in your hearing." — Luke 4:21b

Global Mission

In this day and age it is terribly important that we emphasize in our parishes the fact that we are a global family. Our theology has said this all along, but now because of modern technology and communication, this emphasis is very obvious in nearly every other institution and ought to be especially so in our congregations. The following are 17 ideas I have on making this emphasis quite obvious in a local congregation.

1. Most church denominations have the opportunity for a local congregation to sponsor a unit of a missionary. This usually can be anywhere from a few hundred dollars to the full amount it costs the church to maintain a family in a country other than the United States. Sponsoring one or more units of different missionaries makes it possible to have communication with them and have their names show up in the budget of the congregation and on the congregation's letterhead, thus sensitizing the congregation to the work of missions and missionaries.

2. Nearly every week in the prayer of the church in our worship service, we ought to remember one of our sister congregations around the world and especially those missionaries whom we are sending there. A full listing of the missionaries and the areas where they serve can be found in most national church directories.

3. Be sure to organize a task force in your parish that has the responsibility of emphasizing global ministries. This need not be large, and can be made up of three or four people. Often folks who travel and already have a global perspective make the best members for this.

4. Don't miss the opportunity to serve as a tour guide and take a group of your members to one of the areas where we provide missionaries or mission help. Often the leader of the group can travel free if they recruit five or six to take the

tour. There are travel agencies that work at this; check them out for reputation, results, etc. Some have not produced what was expected.

5. Many denominations provide mission events each summer which are very popular. Usually they meet in several locations across the United States on university campuses. Rent a van (if your church doesn't have one) for a group of your people and attend yourself. They are marvelous, family-oriented events where you can meet many of the missionaries and attend "free university."

6. Every denomination has returned or retired missionaries who are available to speak in congregations. These are often very interesting people who can provide a lot of information in the pulpit, adult forums and at evening potluck suppers or other congregational gatherings. One warning: missionaries often preach too long and if they show slides or videos they can go on forever! Just tactfully explain the time limits and they will comply. See to it that an honorarium is paid and that housing, transportation and so forth is agreed on advance.

7. If you call your nearest church college or seminary, you will find that they all contain international students who are willing to come to the parish for a weekend and preach, speak, show pictures and meet with individual groups. This is a nice event where you show them your community and congregation and in turn learn about their culture and country.

8. It's not too difficult to set up a pen pal system. In my own parish I was always able to set up pen pals through the confirmation class and also some of the members of the women's organization. A warning here would be not to expect answers right away from all missionaries who are addressed by letter from your congregation. In many countries this isn't as easy as it is to do in the United States!

9. You can enrich your ministry by taking a three months' sabbatical and serving as a volunteer in one of the areas where your church is a partner in mission. In most denominations a division for global mission or similar division will coordinate this and delight in helping you get connected with those local, indigenous churches.

10. Try using the church's media, such as videos provided on global mission interpretation. You can subscribe to your denomination's magazine which has a global mission emphasis.

11. It's fun to organize a mission night and make it intergenerational, with foods from various countries. Let the family or people who provide a special food that evening describe the country and our mission work there.

12. Some adult church school classes like to study the areas in which their denomination is involved in missions. Most denominations will provide the material necessary to carry on a six- to eight-week course.

13. In the church bulletin and newsletter it's very easy to include a paragraph now and then about a particular missionary's activities or a particular country where we, in tandem with the national church, do mission together. Be sure not to write these paragraphs in a condescending way and be sure to emphasize that we now do mission on six continents in an interdependent way.

14. Hold an annual mission Sunday. You may be able to initiate global mission staff from the churchwide office of your denomination to speak and preach. It's a good time to have church school classes make flags of the countries where we share mission work, encourage the task force to sponsor a meal after the worship services which have foods from various countries, and invite local college students or anyone you might find available from that country within driving distance.

15. It is important to have a line item in your congregational budget for a specific national church mission. This holds up before the congregation the importance of mission and lets them see that we are, indeed, a global community. It gives "a face" to a ministry.

16. If people in your congregation are willing to house a youth or missionary for a period of time and let that be known to your global mission department, you can have a great experience that will influence the whole congregation. Those in charge of global mission interpretation will provide good bulletin inserts which ought to be used frequently.

17. I found it very effective to purchase a large map of the world, drill holes where your church does mission work and string Christmas lights that blink in each of those holes. This calls attention to how your denomination is a global family and where we work and cooperate together.

The Reverend Arthur Bauer has written a little book called *Making Mission Happen*. Written while Art was the mission interpreter for the Division for World Mission and Ecumenism of the Lutheran Church in America, this is the best book I have found yet to provide ideas on how to stress locally the importance of missions.

Perhaps the most exciting ministry you can perform in the area of global mission is to frequently announce the volunteer opportunities available through the national church to serve six months, a year, two years, three years, in mission work in another country. The congregation can get very excited about sending a single person, a couple, or a youth somewhere in the world to serve the church as a voluntary missionary.

These are some ideas I think of and which I have used and found to work very well in getting the congregation to look outside itself and the United States to begin to envision a larger world and Christian community of brothers and sisters. This seems so consistent with what I believe Christ would have us do in this day when we can communicate and travel with such ease all around the world and get to know others of God's people.

When To Leave The Parish:

Signs It's Time To Move On

When To Leave The Parish

While flying on United flight #1416 from Los Angeles to Oakland, the following came to mind as guidelines for helping pastors decide when to leave a parish ministry for a new call or retirement:

When that inevitable new call comes, you must actually consider two calls: the one under which you have been living and serving, and the new one being presented to you. When the new call seems to be much stronger than the present one, it may be time to move. When a new congregation obviously needs the kind of skills and abilities you have to do the kingdom work, that is another indication it may be time to leave. When people you respect advise or encourage you to move on from your present ministry, you need to consider that advice seriously, along with the opinions of other responsible people. Pastor Don Hillerich reminds me that our dean at Hamma School of Theology, Elmer Flack, used to say: "You owe it to the Holy Spirit to at least talk to the people who have approached you."

There are four major signs to look for when it's time to leave: 1) when you find that mentally it is no longer possible to love the congregation; 2) when you find yourself at loggerheads about what the mission of the congregation is; 3) when your vision for ministry there has dimmed; and 4) when your presence is causing dissension in the present congregation and it is really impossible to mend, or if remaining pastor there will, or has, divided the present staff or the congregation.

Other signs may also suggest looking elsewhere. No matter how good a ministry you have been carrying out, sometimes circumstances indicate that a congregation is ready for a new and different vision and style of leadership. In other instances, in order to snap a congregation out of its passivity, a change in leadership is called for. If you find that a personality cult is developing around you and if, in the minds of many, it is becoming "your" church rather than "our Lord's," you have yet another indication to move on. Sometimes you have done everything you can think of in your ministry and yet there seem to be no positive results. You feel like you just don't know what to do next or how to bring about an effective ministry in that place. Perhaps God's spirit is saying that you have done all you could under the present call and that it is time to consider a new one.

When, in your prayers, God speaks and it's clear you should go, you can do no other. Finding a new challenge and a sense of mission in this new ministry can give you and the new congregation life. It can also provide for the congregation you leave new insight and leadership with new vision, which is often needed.

Pastor Wong claims: "In my experience, when I have had doubts about my call, God responds with the needed affirmation." Sometimes you are blessed when God gives special signs that you ought to go or stay. Being devout in prayer and in your own spiritual life will make you sensitive to these serendipitous signals.

There will be times in your ministry when you have pretty well brought the congregation as far as you can and as far as your vision for their ministry goes. At that time your sense of mission may become dissipated. Your call should be the very thing that would renew and revive you and the congregation where you are going, as well as the one you are leaving.

It is time to leave when you over-identify with the congregation. Some signs of over-identification are these:

1. When you see criticisms as threatening rather than as opportunities to improve.

2. When you get so close to employees and associates that you lose your objectivity as a supervisor.

3. When you fail to take days off and vacations convinced the place can't go on without you.

4. When you just can't see anything deficient in your parish and take every suggestion of deficiency as a personal criticism.

5. When you begin to resent those who disagree with you and crave gratitude rather than respectful disagreement.

When you no longer have the energy to go the extra mile or carry out the heavy routine of parish ministry in your present location, that could indicate you are depressed and discouraged. When your ministry becomes that kind of burden, you need to take intentional steps to change the circumstances, such as taking a sabbatical or continuing education course, adding staff, or sharing the problem with a pastoral relations committee. Another method is accepting a new call.

One bishop advised me that it's time to accept a new call "when you are rounding first base and just don't want to slide into second." That bishop no doubt meant that you are no longer willing to "pay the price" for a vital ministry.

It also may be important to move from your present parish if your retirement would make way for new and vigorous leadership and you no longer feel you can provide that. Stepping aside is then a godly and graceful thing to do.

There are a number of reasons that might cause you to move to a new parish which are not really valid. If your attitude is one of "I'll get even" or "I'll show them," or that "they'll appreciate me when I am gone," then you don't have a very valid reason for leaving the present situation. To avoid being over-involved and overworked is not a good reason either. That same situation will develop rapidly in the new parish.

If you are accepting a new call simply to avoid the painful process of conflict resolution or to escape the embarrassment of mistakes you have made, the next parish call will probably not go any better. Pastor Winkel states: "There may be a call leading us to consider a new vocation outside of parish ministry. To multiply mistakes and disappointments and anger by moving to a new parish is not always a solution or a response to a 'call.' " It is not good to leave just to get a higher salary or to live in a certain preferential area, either. Nor should you leave the parish in order to use your already-delivered sermons over again!

Occasionally a pastor will leave the parish in order to compensate for a loss, such as the death of a loved one, or disappointment by children, or some other cause for grief. In most cases it is not wise to go to a new call until the grief work has been completed.

Listen to our lay person, Anna-Marie Klein, as she gives her opinion on when to leave: "Pastors stay sometimes for their own sakes and it hurts to leave the parish. This is hard to face. In my opinion, eight to ten years is long enough for a pastor to remain in a parish unless the pastor has an unusually large quantity of skills. Even in parishes with other staff, the eight to ten years is the time for change. Pastors sometimes act as though they are the only ones needing to move. In the workplace today, however upsetting, many move all the time. Church growth might be enhanced if pastors moved more.

"When a pastor is in one parish a long time the personality of the pastor and ministry often become the same. When the pastor does move, transition is difficult."

Pastor Robert Hock, who has been in the same parish for 21 years and has led a very dynamic ministry, writes: ". . . say it's okay to stay longer too! The church needs more longer stays as pastors."

After all is said and done, the best reason to accept a new call, after much prayer, is because you just can't resist it! It is attractive, it is fascinating, you can't get it out of your mind, and God makes it irresistible.

Sometimes people with spiritual depth in the new parish will be absolutely convinced that God has led them to you. This should not be taken lightly. Church leaders you respect may be certain you are the best person and the match is right between you and a congregation. Because the church bureaucrat and bishop often have the larger picture of both congregations in mind, their advice is invaluable.

Often receiving a new call, even though you turn it down, can bring a renewed vigor and sense of mission in your present call. When calls come right after the other, that may be a strong indication that you have the kind of skills and spiritual depth much needed in many congregations, and it could also mean that it is time to depart from where you have served.

Thus ends our "plane thoughts" about parish ministry. In response to the captain's admonishment to "prepare the cabin for landing," the flight attendant announces, "Seatbacks in their upright positions, tray tables stowed, seat belts fastened and any hand baggage under the seat in front of you." We will complete our flight plan for being an effective pastor. As we reach the time when the plane is "committed" to the runway, I'm hopeful these insights from many, many flights will be worthwhile to all of us who fill the office of pastor. Paul is right: "God in God's mercy has given us this ministry, and so we do not become discouraged." — 2 Corinthians 4:1

Joyous take offs, purposeful travel and confident landing to us all!

Recommended Reading

Bringing Your Church Back to Life: Beyond Survival Mentality, by Daniel Buttry, Judson Press, 1989.

Good advice on moving a congregation from a survival mentality to a new vision for ministry and mission.

Giving and Stewardship in an Effective Church, by Kennon L. Callahan, Harper Collins, 1993.

This is the no-nonsense, close-to-the-ground approach to financial stewardship in the parish.

The Steward: A Biblical Symbol Come of Age, by Douglas John Hall, Eerdmans/Friendship Press, 1990.

Here is an expansive view of stewardship as lifestyle affecting all of life in the pastor's life and in the parish.

Pastor as Person, by Gary L. Harbaugh, Augsburg Publishing House, 1984.

This book deals with real life issues for clergy such as stress, dependency, anger, feelings and commitment. It deals with the dilemmas of being a person who is also a pastor.

Pastoral Spirituality: A Focus for Ministry, by Ben Campbell Johnson, Westminster Press, 1988.

Practical suggestions for regaining and maintaining our spiritual health in the role of parish pastor.

Effective Church Leadership, by Harris W. Lee, Augsburg/Minneapolis, 1989.

Good practical ideas on pastoral leadership written by one who has been there. It contains a number of excellent tools for evaluating our leadership style.

The Once and Future Church, by Loren B. Mead, Alban Institute, 1991.

Here is a vision of congregational mission in the next century. It will challenge parish leaders to seek new paradigms for ministry in their context.

Contemporary Images of Christian Ministry, by Donald E. Messer, Abingdon Press, 1989.

New and visionary ways of looking at our task as parish pastors.

The Evangelical Pastor, by Mark A. Olson, Augsburg Fortress, 1992.

A refreshing look at the leadership of the pastor (far beyond enabler) for a witnessing congregation.

Forty-four Ways to Expand the Teaching Ministry of Your Church, by Lyle Schaller, Abingdon Press, 1993.

A book full of practical suggestions and "how tos" in programming the parish to do education that is meaningful to our present culture.

Called To Witness, by Jerry L. Schmalenberger, CSS, Lima, Ohio, 1993.

A manual for congregational outreach and growth.

Testing and Reclaiming Your Call to Ministry, by Robert Schnase, Abingdon Press, 1991.

A number of ways to keep the call alive and our ministry vigorous.

Sex in the Forbidden Zone, by Peter Rutter, M.D., Jeremy P. Tarcher, Inc. 1989.

Here are insights into erotically charged relationships, especially male abuse of women. An important book for these sexualized times.